PAST PERFECT

Christine Noble

PAST PERFECT:
FROM CURSES TO BLESSINGS

MarshallPickering

An Imprint of HarperCollins*Publishers*

First published in Great Britain in 1991 by Marshall Pickering
Marshall Pickering is an imprint of
HarperCollinsReligious
Part of HarperCollinsPublishers
77-85 Fulham Palace Road, London W6 8JB

Printed and bound in Great Britain
by HarperCollins Manufacturing

Scripture quotations are taken from the *New International Version
Bible* copyright © 1973, 1978, 1984, by the International Bible
Society. Used by permission of Hodder and Stoughton.

Contents

Acknowledgements

Thank you, John, for helping me stick with it to the end. Thanks to my daughter Ruth for the hours of typing and retyping. Thanks to Stuart Murray for keeping me on the straight and narrow.

Receive it. I hope is that every member will help in…
people as they… will spurt to get there before Christ's
now fresh

Michael Hart

Foreword

Many years ago I heard a German called Wilhard Becker give a talk on "blessing and cursing". It made a deep impression on me, and I have never forgotten what he said.

I thought it would be good one day to develop the theme myself, not only in talks, but in a book. Thankfully I won't now have to do it, because Christine Noble has done such a good job!

It can be frightening to realize that a few words can save a person, and equally a few words can destroy someone. No wonder Jesus said that we will one day be judged by what we say, as well as by what we do. How often I have regretted words I have said, and words I have failed to say! Equally, how good it has been to hear that words spoken, often unawares, have changed the course of people's lives.

I met John and Christine for the first time in 1958. I found them difficult people then. They seemed to question everything! But they were real seekers, and one of the great joys of my life has been to see what has come from those beginnings, and the fruit that has been gathered. This book is another fruit, and it is a pleasure to write this

foreword. I hope as they read it the book will help many
people to allow the Holy Spirit to use their lips for blessing
not cursing.

Michael Harper

Introduction

There is great confusion and ignorance amongst Christians when it comes to blessings and curses. Opinions range from total absorption with one or the other, to almost complete disbelief that we can experience either this side of eternity. With the rise of interest in the supernatural realm, both in the church and society, it is essential that we understand how blessings and curses affect our lives. The Bible and our experience should be in harmony in teaching us the lessons. I trust my book will provide some of the answers and throw light on areas which you may never have considered before. Prophets of doom and gloom, the prosperity cult, triumphalists and New Age infiltration are among the influences which are beginning to affect the thinking of people in our churches. We must not withdraw into a defensive mode, full of fear and reaction, or we will leave the arena clear for the enemy to do his will unhindered. We must arm ourselves with faith and knowledge and move out to combat the enemy's strategy.

Faced with the subject of cursing and blessing, we will all want to embrace blessing and steer clear of curses. We all desire to experience blessings from the hand of our heavenly Father and also from one another. Cursing, however, is a very different kettle of fish. Who wants to even think about it, let alone experience it? Some may feel it is a subject which, as Christians, we shouldn't mention – in fact, if you ignore it, it may go away altogether. Others consider cursing to be an outmoded subject for us – something from the realm of the heathen, superstition, voodoo and black magic, and certainly not something relevant to a God of love or to his people. Some dismiss the topic as having been dealt with by the sacrifice of Jesus, along with sickness, demons and death. Of course, this is absolutely true. We have to admit, however, that the truth is not always a reality in our lives in any of these areas, so we cannot just disregard them and bury our heads in the sand.

To over-react is, in my opnion, firstly, to lose some of the impact from the blessings which are poured out into our lives, by God, our families and our friends. Secondly, we can become closed by fear to the possibility of a curse in our lives, which may have a stultifying or harmful effect in our family, our work for the Lord or our walk with him. Thirdly, without the ability to either curse or bless, we are deficient. You may immediately feel that you don't particularly want to be able to curse, and perhaps you are a little embarrassed at the idea of blessing someone or something. If these are your reactions, then already you've lost out and become the poorer for it. We need to be able to clearly and soundly curse the work of Satan in people's lives, in society's structures and wherever we find it. We also need to be those who can say, "Well done" or "I love you, my son, my daughter" or "May God bless your work for him". By showing our interest, love and support towards what God is doing in the lives of others, we become agents dispensing God's blessings.

Introduction

Our language has many pairs of words which express obvious opposites. To delete or weaken one word is to devalue its power of contrast. Consider for a moment how you would explain the concept and movement involved in the simple word, "up" if you didn't also have its counterpart, "down". The same is true of hot and cold, ugly and beautiful, clever and stupid, strong and weak, and many more. We somehow lose the depth of meaning and power from both words when we change the value of one. The same, then, is true of other pairs of words, such as sin and righteousness, wounds and healing, rejection and acceptance, good and evil, curse and blessing. How we need these contrasts to help us to understand the depths of God's love and the enormous price Christ paid for each one of us! The cross on which Jesus hung is the overwhelming example of this. The Lord was suspended between earth and heaven; both had rejected him utterly in that moment, so that we might be accepted. Without that terrible rejection, God's incredible acceptance of us is impossible. In the same way, understanding the awful pain of the curse helps us to appreciate the tremendous value of the blessing.

The world accepts, in a matter-of-fact way, the curses which run through some people's lives and through whole families at times. Much is attributed to luck, both good and bad, in the purely human order of things. Without Christ people have no way out – they are helpless to change things. The blessings of God, and the strength and life which they bring, are outside of the experience of the majority of mankind. Tragically, the same is true for many Christians. We fail to understand what is in God's heart for us. Because of this we are slow to appreciate his blessings, and even slower in owning up to the curses in our lives, and allowing him to deal with them. Let us therefore give some thought and prayer to this whole subject. There will almost certainly be some cause for action as we, the people of God, become doers of the word as a result of being hearers of the word. Let's go forward with the Holy Spirit in order to illuminate our understanding.

PART I
CURSES

1

The significance of words

And God said, "Let there be light," and there was light.
                                                    Genesis 1:3

The words we speak hold great significance both for ourselves and for our hearers. We don't actually give sufficient weight to the power which words have to bless and to curse. In today's world we use words to negotiate and turn situations to our advantage. This means that when someone places an advertisement in a newspaper to sell an item, everyone knows that the seller will take less than the price requested. Sometimes the letters "o.n.o." (meaning "or near offer") are added; in other words, our sale price is not really a true one. We have learned to live with this and to adjust our thinking to it, but this is not how God sees words at all.

When the Lord said, "Let us make man in our image," that was precisely what he intended. Halfway through creation he didn't say, "What I really meant by that was, 'Let us make someone similar to but not exactly like us.'" He meant what he said, and still does today. Because we are made in his image, he demands that same attitude from us – he expects us to mean what we say. That is quite a responsibility; we need to guard our words far more than we do.

Three men once came to see my husband John. They were late arriving, and we had a very tight schedule. At one point I knocked on the door and said, "Love, we should have left twenty minutes ago." "Thanks," said John, not looking as if he intended to make a move. "We'd better be on our way," one of the guys said, "or you'll get a lot more words than that when we leave." John was able to say, "No I won't. Christine has made her statement, and that's it." It struck me then, as it often has, how people (particularly women) use words to nag. That was really what was inferred on this occasion. The expectation of our visitor was that there must be much more to come, all probably negative. We use words to manipulate other people, not quite telling them what we really have in mind, breaking them in gently to our own hidden agenda.

We ask questions, already having decided the answer we want to receive. "Do you like my new coat? Do you think it suits me?" "Yes! Yes!" is what we want to hear. "What must I do to be your disciple?" asked the rich young ruler of Jesus. "Sell everything" was not the reply he had anticipated, and he went away sad, knowing he had heard the truth.

On the other hand, there are some amongst us who pride themselves on speaking out. These types tell you the unvarnished truth as they see it. This also has an effect on the hearer. "You don't look too good today," they will tell you. "Oh, I feel fine," you reply. "It must be that terrible colour you're wearing, then. I never have liked it." With this kind of encouragement we could be tempted never to wear the garment again, or perhaps we will feel uncomfortable every time we put it on.

The truth seldom fully coincides with your point of view. Nor is the truth simply facts; it's a person – Jesus! He said, "I am the way, the truth and the life." We must release him into our lives and the lives of those who seek him, if the truth is to set us free.

"If you really love me, you'll tell me the secret of your strength," wheedled Delilah. The result of this emotional blackmail led Samson to the grinding stone. "If you really love me, you'll empty the pedal bin" or ". . . not worry if I'm out late" or ". . . trust me". This sort of thing can lead to real problems. Words have a power to confuse or clarify, to bring light or murky darkness. God stands by the words he utters; he also stands by our words. In Matthew 27:25 we read that the Jews cursed themselves. Pilate had just declared that he was innocent of the blood of Jesus, and the people answered him, "Let his blood be on us and on our children!" The history of the Jewish nation bears witness to this curse continuing throughout the generations. God recorded their words, which stand until they humble themselves and seek his forgiveness.

People curse themselves, without any concept of the effect it will have in their lives. One lonely girl I was able to help used to look in the mirror and say, "I wish I'd never been born." What a terrible curse this was. She finally came to the point where she could not look at herself at all, and was convinced that God could never use her. I have seen many people gain repentance and freedom from cursing themselves. The results of belittling ourselves in this way take many forms, from anorexia and bulimia, through to self-mutilation and suicide. What we are implying, in effect, when we say this kind of thing is that God didn't know what he was doing when he made us. Words are indeed powerful, but as with every other transgression, their misuse can be dealt with and forgiven.

Read: Psalm 139:13-16; John 8:31-36 & 18:37-40; Matthew 27:11-26.

Consider and pray: Have you, even inadvertently, cursed yourself or someone else with ill-chosen words? If so, acknowledge this before the Lord and receive his forgiveness and release. You will find yourself entering into a whole new realm of peace and freedom with him. Others who have suffered from the effects of your tongue need the benefit of hearing your confession and repentance and being able to personally forgive you.

2
Word power

May the words of my mouth and the meditation of my heart be pleasing in your sight, O Lord, my Rock and my Redeemer.

Psalm 19:14

Then Jacob called for his sons and said: "Gather around so I can tell you what will happen to you in days to come."

Genesis 49:1

The old children's chant "Sticks and stones may break my bones, but names will never hurt me" is just not always true. There are many occasions when words immediately cause immense suffering and pain. Sometimes there are shock reactions, and even fatality may be the result. However, usually it is the long-term effects which are more serious. Surely every one of us nurses some hurt in this respect.

As we have already seen, words have a value and force within themselves. They are used to communicate thoughts, ideas, feelings and desires from one person to another, one group to another, one nation to another.

Frequently they are prophetic and carry seeds that will come to maturity and will even continue to produce harvests throughout the years. Jacob's blessing of his twelve sons is a great testimony to this, as his words continue to be worked out through the history of the tribes of Israel.

As well as the Lord hearing what we say, Satan and demons also pick up our words and work with them. When we take this into account, the results of the spoken word can be shattering. We don't need to look very far to substantiate this claim – only as far as our television screens. After the invasion of Kuwait, Saddam Hussein's speech to his nation about the build-up of United Nations forces on his border had an immediate and visible effect. His followers began to ritually beat their breasts in response to his words. He incited the crowds in much the same way as Hitler did. As we look down through history, we have innumerable examples of this same power let loose through words. We have Elizabeth I inspiring men to explore new, uncharted seas and lands, and we have Churchill and his rallying speeches during World War II. In the same way we are moved by literature and inspired by songs. They have the power to affect us and to change the course of our lives.

We therefore have a responsibility to choose the correct words to convey our meaning. Our feelings are often expressed in a quick outburst which, on reflection, wasn't what we wanted to convey at all. How many times have we been in the position of wishing that we could take back our words? Words, then, have great power over their hearers. The child on the receiving end of a torrent of words from a parent about how clumsy, stupid, bad or uncooperative he is must surely be affected by them. Tell that child regularly enough that he is thick, and he will begin to believe it.

Frequently I have listened to children and adults who have been abused. The greatest hurdle for them to over-come is the personal sense of blame. Part of the recurring pattern is that the abuser has repeatedly said, "Don't tell anyone – this has to be our secret. If you do tell, people will think you are a bad boy or girl." Through such words the whole responsibility has been shifted from the guilty party onto the innocent child. The power of these words is multiplied when the abuser is a close relation – a father, mother or brother – because of the bonding of love in the family. These curses need to be formally broken through the power of Jesus Christ, so that the person can become free and healed from the pain.

Just as curses have power, so blessings do also. In our culture we are reserved and tend to shy away from overtly encouraging one another. When your child brings his or her first drawing to you, if you are unwise you might say, "What on earth is that?" Thankfully most parents don't do that; they would say, "It's lovely, darling." Obviously, if your offspring is still scribbling at fifteen you need to encourage them into other areas where they are gifted and away from drawing entirely. Generally speaking, we do not bless and encourage one another nearly enough. Teachers will tell you that they can see a remarkable difference in the classroom between the child whose parents regularly say, "Well done!" and the child who is put down.

At the end of our wedding day, as we were leaving the reception, my father shook my new husband by the hand and said, "I'll give you six months." What a blight to be placed upon us at the beginning of our marriage! I can explain the reasoning behind his words. He knew me and had some knowledge of John, so he knew that two very strong people were coming together. He could see little hope for our future. His words bore fruit; our marriage did founder. But, praise God, there was something he had left out of the equation – the Lord! Jesus came into our lives and broke the power of that curse, and John and I fell in love all over again.

In Genesis there are many examples of spoken words which bear fruit. Sometimes people uttered them without fully understanding what the outcome would be. Jacob gained a blessing through deceit and subterfuge, and his father could not recall it. The words had been spoken; they would be effective down the years. Rachel was Jacob's favourite wife, but without realizing it he cursed her with death. He was unaware that she had her father's household gods hidden away when he cursed the one who had stolen them. Later Rachel died in childbirth, fulfilling the words which he had spoken.

We certainly need to take stock of everything we say. Idle talk and thoughts set off chain reactions. As the Lord brings things to mind, we need to repent and take the appropriate action. Speak to your children, your spouse, your relatives and your friends, asking for their forgiveness. Set them free and break the bondage you have imposed, however unthinkingly. Be generous with your blessings and encouragements and do battle with your reticence, which might itself even be the result of your history. You men, show affection to your sons and to your brothers in Christ. Kick the fear of being considered soft and unmanly; this fear can cause families to drift apart. Jesus if far more powerful than the inhibitions which surface in us. We are to be mature sons and daughters, able to accept the responsibility of giving and receiving forgiveness.

Read: Psalm 59:6-13; Psalm 64.

Consider and pray: In the last section I asked you to think about the words you have said about yourself and others. Continue to ask the Holy Spirit to highlight past areas of weakness. Repent and release anyone you may have hurt in this way, particularly members of your own family. Maybe you yourself have suffered from such treatment as a child at home or in school, or as an adult in your work. This kind of misuse of words can effectively curse you and prevent your free expression. Pray for yourself and if necessary seek the help of wise and trusted Christian friends. Break the power which those inhibiting words have had over you, and see your freedom complete.

3
Where it all began

"Cursed is the ground because of you; through painful toil you will eat of it all the days of your life. It will produce thorns and thistles for you, and you will eat the plants of the field. By the sweat of your brow you will eat your food until you return to the ground, since from it you were taken; for dust you are and to dust you will return."

Genesis 3:17-19

This clearly is a curse placed by God upon the environment, and therefore directly upon mankind. So the Creator himself is in the business of cursing his creation. Until this moment in time, the garden of Eden had held only blessings for Adam and Eve. They had been placed into ideal circumstances. The weather was perfect – so much so that they didn't need clothes or coverings to keep them warm. They could explore every aspect of nature, as there was no fear between them and the animals, nor between the animals themselves. It was indeed paradise, a place the world only dreams of today. What happened, then, to smash the picture, to bring about pain where there had only been joy?

Here at the very beginning of human history we see God's heart towards man. His fatherly love shows in the care he weaves into creation. No thorns and thistles to choke the plants; no merciless sun to scorch the life from the earth; no deluge of water to sweep away the topsoil, leaving devastation in its wake. This was a place we can only imagine, perfect for man, nature and animals; an environment of complete harmony, where we could walk with God, enjoy his friendship and love one another. That was our heavenly Father's desire for us. Just a few simple rules were given by the Creator of this wonderful paradise, so that we could gain the maximum benefit from it all. "Freely enjoy the fruit from any tree but one. Eat that and you will die. Be fruitful yourselves and multiply." All that blessing, all that freedom! God did not want us to die and return to dust; he wanted us to live.

Mankind just had to prove for themselves that that certain fruit would poison them and that God's promises were absolutely true. Eating the fruit did indeed kill them, and God had no choice but to uphold the single law he had given them, in order to allow freewill to function. How it must have hurt to punish us. Parents experience this in a measure, themselves. We don't want to hurt our children, but sometimes we have only the choice between doing nothing, which is bad parenting, and discipline. Perhaps we are guilty at times of making bad decisions, but God never is. He is the perfect Father.

So, the Lord brought judgment into the world because of our sin. He cursed the earth and death became part of our everyday experience. Did he have to be so severe? After all, it was our very first misdemeanour. But the fact is that it only takes one sin to separate us from God. In

Genesis 3:22 we see that he was even good enough to explain his actions. There was in the garden another tree, the "tree of life". The fruit of this tree brought immortality, and it was not forbidden. God obviously intended us to find it in our explorations and walks with him. Then we would eat from it and live forever. Death was not part of his plan. However, once we had been disobedient he could not allow us to find and eat of that tree, for then we would have lived for ever in a fallen state.

How we have misjudged God and hurt him over the centuries with our warped view and lack of understanding. The cry still goes up to him today, "If you really are a God of love, how can you be party to the suffering of people's lives?" How can he not be, when he has given us the free will with which to choose life, and yet we continue to choose the tree of the knowledge of good and evil and therefore death?

Even here, in the midst of all the pain, God still shows his love and concern for us. He must exclude us from the garden but he gives us hope, he gives a promise (Genesis 3:15). A son is to be born from the woman, and he will put an end to evil. Although Adam and Eve were expelled from Eden, they could look down the years to that son who was to come – the Messiah, Saviour of the world. God did not leave creation in the lurch; he provided a way back to himself. In the church, we look back to that central point in history and receive the promise of everlasting life. Space does not permit me to deal with all of God's curses in the garden and their effects throughout history. However, I have covered them in my book, *What in the world is God saying about women?* published by Kingsway. Can I encourage you to read it?

Read: Genesis 3:1-24; Romans 8:18-27.

Consider and pray: As man is directly responsible for the curse upon nature, we should be concerned to care for the world in which we live. Because we can't be involved in every area related to the corruption of our planet, most of us do nothing. This must change. We can all begin to pray and from this base become active in those things which God puts on our hearts.

Death also entered into that perfect garden as a result of our sin. In the light of this, we should be seeking ways to bring the message of life to those who are still under that sentence of death. As you pray today, ask the Lord to remove apathy and fear, the two great hindrances to action.

Introduction to meditations four to nine

Deuteronomy 27:14-26 deals with God's curses upon his own people. I will be dividing this scripture into five principal sections, which we will consider in the next six meditations. The first section is concerned with God's rule in our lives, without any idols or images; the second with our attitude towards fellow believers; the third with our treatment of the underprivileged and unbelievers; the fourth with our family behaviour and morals; and the fifth with hatred and violence. Obviously these areas overlap, and whilst the different aspects are important, my prime concern is to draw from you a personal response to God.

4
No other gods!

The Levites shall recite to all the people of Israel in a loud voice: "Cursed is the man who carves an image or casts an idol – a thing detestable to the Lord, the work of craftsmen's hands – and sets it up in secret." Then shall all the people say, "Amen!"

Deuteronomy 27:14-15

So much is wrapped up in these two verses which is applicable to us today. This statement was made by a jealous God, who was not willing to share the throne of our hearts with anyone or anything. Down the years, in spite of man's initial and continuing sin in turning his back on his Creator, the Lord's aims and objectives have not changed. He was and is still looking for a people who will keep his commandments, become his friends, work with him to bring about the kingdom of heaven upon earth and never physically die. At no time has he given up on his plan, regardless of all our grousing about him, our misunderstanding of his goals and objectives and our ignoring his very existence. Even when we killed his beloved Son, he never changed his heart towards us.

In the scripture above the Levites of the time were speaking to people who had recently come out of Egypt. They had lived there for generations and had absorbed the culture as well as many of the religious practices. One of the things which the Lord hates and will not allow is a mixture. He will not allow any heathen practices amongst his people. We are either for him or against him. We are unacceptable if we are lukewarm, and for this offence he will vomit us up or remove the candlestick of our testimony. He wants us to be hot for him, ready to be hearers and doers of his word. If we are cold, it is clear where we stand, but the lukewarm are detestable to God. What, then, is he cursing in these verses?

Well, he certainly isn't saying that we should destroy all sculpture, art, china figures and wall plaques, along with their designers. The ability to create beautiful things comes under the heading of blessing – but more of that later. What, then, is God speaking about? He is referring to anything or anyone who becomes to us as important as, or even more important than, our heavenly Father. When this happens they become objects of worship and superstition, taking the place of God in our lives.

God's chosen people were riddled with idolatry. They had their own household gods, they had taken on the moral and cultural practices of the Egyptians, and at times they worshipped the temple gods. They were in the Lord's eyes a polluted mixture. He wanted to bless them and use them to bless all the nations of the earth, but there had to be a clean-up and clear-out first. Things have changed very little over the centuries. God is still looking to bless the world, but now through the church, which is made up of believers from all nations. She too is riddled with these

same practices, albeit under different guises. So the curse
is still applicable to us today. God wants to show us exactly
what they are and how these things have infiltrated our
lives, in order to release us from his curse. He is a good and
loving Father, but he is unable to coexist with other gods.

What are today's idols? They certainly won't be new
ones – just the old ones with a new coat of paint. There are
our own aims and objectives – perhaps academic achieve-
ment, world travel, a healthy body, a big church, success
in business, happiness, wealth. It may well be in God's
plan for us to have some and perhaps all of those things,
but he won't share our hearts with them. For instance, he
would rather that we never left our native land than that he
should have to share us with world travel.

Another idol contending for the throne may be one of a
number of fears. We fear growing old, getting fat, dying,
loneliness, being out of control, criticism, water, heights
and making decisions. There are many, many more.
Whilst these fears are present the Lord cannot have us all
to himself. Perhaps he may be relegated to a lower position, rather than being in the number one spot in our lives.

Perhaps, as in the past, the Asherah pole or Dagon
rules. Old-fashioned names, but nevertheless quite relevant even today, as Christians can be found involved in
occult practices. Astrologers and fortune-tellers now ply
their trade on our TV screens. Spiritualism is a growing
religion. It has been misnamed the "Christian Spiritualist
Church". There can't possibly be such a thing; Chris-
tianity and spiritualism are diametrically opposed. True
Christians give place only to the Holy Spirit, spiritualists
to many false and lying spirits. How many people in the
church of Jesus Christ are still tainted with these and other
similar practices? Freemasonry and most secret societies
number believers amongst their members. The dictionary

definition of "occult" is "magical, mystical, mysterious, something that comes between". If you read your horoscope, it subtly comes between you and God. You don't need such things, as your future is secure in him. If you are giving your allegiance to any secret society, however much that society is projected as being benign, it comes between you and God. We have the knowledge of an open secret. We have the free gift of life everlasting through Jesus Christ our Lord. Think seriously: is God speaking to you about some specific idol? Listen to the Holy Spirit and dethrone everything except the Almighty Father and his Son, Jesus.

Read: 1 John 5:13-21.

Consider and pray: Every vestige of false worship and every hint of other gods must be rejected. No superstition of any kind must be allowed to coexist with Jesus. Feelings of well-being must not dictate to us what we believe; only God's word should be allowed to do that. Whatever we feel like, Jesus Christ died for our sins, and he wants to deal with deceiving fears and feelings. Bring them to him, confessing the power they have held over you. If you are in any doubt, ask for help from someone in leadership who is experienced in this area.

5

Mammon

No-one can serve two masters. Either he will hate the one and love the other, or he will be devoted to the one and despise the other. You cannot serve both God and Money.

Matthew 6:24

A final word from me on the subject of who or what is on the throne of our lives. There is an idol which is strong and deadly and yet sometimes difficult to recognise. It is certainly difficult to deal with. This particular poison has become so much part and parcel of our lives in the affluent West that we are unaware of its grip. I'm talking about materialism – or Mammon, as the Bible calls it! We have looked across at the Eastern Bloc countries and have bewailed their lack of personal freedom, the dearth of products in their shops and the poor state of their national economies. We have likened communism to a great bear, with its encircling arms slowly but surely crushing people to death. All of which is true; personal liberty on every front has been restricted, and for many it has been forcibly removed. But are we so much better off under capitalism here in the West?

Things are very different in our democracies. We have freedom of choice – in fact, multiple choices. Our shops are full of desirable goods, from shoes to refrigerators. Our enemy is less obvious than communism; it is like a cancer, growing slowly but surely inside. It is just as deadly as the bear, but it is hidden and subtle. Perhaps we aren't actually misers, collecting coins in little bags and stacking them under the floorboards. Money itself may not be our obsession; it is far more likely to be the possessions that money can buy. We live in a society which encourages us to feel hard done by if we can't afford this season's fashions, this year's car, double glazing, wine with our meals and so on – the list is endless. As a nation we are in debt up to our eyebrows. Mammon clearly rules in our society. Can we say that the "cancer" is so much better than the "bear"? Surely, what we as Christians need to see is that both are evil systems. The Berlin Wall has come down; people are free from that fear. Satan will not, however, hang around. He will be actively helping people to exchange one form of bondage for another. He doesn't care which form ensnares us; he only looks for slaves, never free men and women.

How does all of this affect you personally? I want to encourage you, with the Spirit's help, to take a long, hard look at your lifestyle. Ask yourself, are you living beyond your income? Are there certain possessions which you just cannot do without? Is there something which fills your horizon and your every thought, so that you are fully convinced that if you had this something you would be truly happy? Could it be the wedding dress of your dreams? The fitted kitchen of your choice? The car you've been looking at recently in the showroom? None of these things in themselves are necessarily wrong for us to own. Sometimes the

Lord does give us material prosperity, but it is not our passport to happiness. Some things we so come to expect that we cease to be grateful to God for them. We take it for granted that they are part of normal living, and if we were to be deprived of them our reactions would be unsanctified, to say the least. The Lord spoke to John and I some time ago about money. We weren't badly in debt, but all the same, we felt he was encouraging us to take a fresh look at our finances. It's so easy for our standards to become gods or idols. I'm so grateful that God spoke to us when he did – otherwise I might be in some difficulty. Let me explain.

We are moving house, as the direct result of a prophetic word from God. I really like my house. It's large and roomy. It's not in a particularly desirable part of town, but it's home. The new area which God has told us to move into is very different – so much so that I'm beginning to feel that the only thing we can afford there might be a garage. Here's the crunch: do we try to match what we now have, or do we take into account what God has said to us about money? The inclination is to match our present home and take on a thumping great mortgage. But we must not do that, even though it is quite a difficult path to walk. Of course, God could drop the money through the letterbox; sometimes he chooses to work that way. On other occasions we just need to learn the lesson and seek to be aware of any erosion that has taken place in our relationship with him. Mostly we need to check the throne to make sure that Jesus is still there alone and not sharing it with a home, a dream holiday, a new food processor, a better music centre, or anything else we might covet.

Read: 2 Peter 2:1-22; 1 Timothy 6:3-10.

Consider and pray: Is the new kitchen or this year's car higher on our agenda than God's work in our city, village or town? Is education and the pursuit of intellectual excellence dictating how much time we have to spend with our brothers and sisters in Christ? Does bettering ourselves put a division between us and the poor? I do not ask these questions to condemn us, only to cause us to be open and honest with God. If we find that, in some way, materialism controls us, then we must heed the words of Jesus and seek first his kingdom. As we do this he will lovingly help us to get our priorities sorted out and to put material things in their rightful place.

6

Respecting boundaries

"Cursed is the man who moves his neighbour's boundary stone." Then all the people shall say, "Amen!"

Deuteronomy 27:17

On the surface, this does seem an unusual thing to be the cause of a curse, but when you look into it more carefully, you see that robbery is involved. There is no need for a detailed explanation of what a boundary stone is; suffice it to say that it marks the extent of the territory under someone's direct control. These lines of ownership can become established in many ways. You might receive a piece of land as a gift, or you might buy it. Entering into marriage establishes a boundary of one particular man or woman in your life. Having children involves new boundaries in the lives of parents. Our natural gifts and talents, given to us by God, are boundaries and limitations, as are our ministries and spiritual gifts. Cursed is the man who takes it upon himself to move or tamper with them. "Then all the people shall say, 'Amen!'"

What could be the motivation for moving these markers, by stealth or trickery or misrepresentation? It could be greed or jealousy or lust. It might be a fear of being outshone and diminished. We need to be extremely careful in our dealings with people, especially if we are leaders in the church, so that we do not fall foul of this particular curse. We also need to be able to help others to identify its influence in their experience. It's no good trying to pretend that the moving of boundaries does not happen amongst Christians, because it most certainly does, and is inevitably the breeding ground of much pain, confusion and disillusionment. Let's look at a few examples of this practice which are taking place in the church today.

Take marriages, for example. When I married John, I settled once and for all on one man. I voluntarily placed clear boundary markers in my life. I took down the sign which stated, "Open to offers" and put up another sign which said, "Taken". How many Christians are shifting boundary stones in this area? The man who wooes another man's wife and the wife who has an affair or is flirtatious can be found too frequently. These sacred boundaries are surely being moved and sometimes moved again and again. This brings God's curse down on our heads, perhaps affecting a family through its generations. This power needs to be smashed through repentance and deliverance, so that such people can be free to love with their boundary stones in place, nicely growing moss.

It's all too easy to stifle children's gifts and abilities. Often it seems that the very naughtiest child in a family is the most talented. We find it hard to encourage the growth of these talents because the child's character is so deplorable. How can we give our "Well done" when, at the same time, our offspring is being rebellious? So we appear to disapprove of the child's whole life, and are guilty of repressing God's gifts.

This also happens in the adult world. Leaders frequently find it difficult or downright impossible to encourage their people and bring discipline at the same time. Others are prejudiced when it comes to certain areas – for example, the arts or entertainment. They demand that people in the more artistic professions, when they come into the family of God, should relinquish their gifts, because they are "suspect". Women too have suffered in this way, even when there are obvious signs of gifting. They can be disqualified from functioning simply by virtue of their gender. Here also we need to take a radical look at what we are doing. If God created specific abilities in women, he has put the markers there, and who are we to say they are null and void? Are we suggesting that God didn't know what he was doing in that particular case?

There are numbers of dispossessed leaders or spiritual fathers and mothers in the church today. They are in no way being honoured, but have been sidelined and in extreme cases "put out of" the very churches they founded and nurtured. Worldly ambition and people having an eye for the main chance have been the motivations in some of these cases. On occasion these sad circumstances have come about through immature, teenage attitudes at the leadership level. These factors have forced boundary changes which are not in line with God's order.

Perhaps another up-to-date example is the way that Christians have been involved in gazumping in house buying and selling. Having several people after your property, each trying to out-bid the others, sounds the ideal scenario if you are selling your home. Surely, once you have agreed a price with a buyer and have given your word, you are guilty of moving the boundaries if you rescind. No wonder that in business today we put everything in writing – and even then we may not be safe. The Bible says we should let our "yes" be "yes" and our "no" be "no" – neither should be "maybe".

Of course, there are many other examples. Right now, as you are reading, the Holy Spirit may be bringing some such situation into your mind. He brings this revelation so that we can get help to turn around and more and more become the people of blessing that God wants us to be.

Read: Philippians 2:3-11.

Consider and pray: God has a purpose and an assignment for each one of us. There is much to be done before the Lord returns and many opportunities. If you lack this sense of purpose and calling, cry out to God, as he positively has a plan for you. He longs for us to cheer one another on in our individual God-given tasks. The world is so large and the need so great that there is no time for jealousy or robbery. Actively pray for the welfare and success of your brothers and sisters in Christ. Respect and honour those whom God has obviously called into leadership, without putting them on a pedestal. Pray too that you might out-do them in love!

7

Justice for the underprivileged

"Cursed is the man who leads the blind astray on the road."
Then all the people shall say, "Amen!" "Cursed is the man
who withholds justice from the alien, the fatherless or the
widow." Then all the people shall say, "Amen!"

Deuteronomy 27:18-19

Silent movies fascinate me. Generally speaking, those old films had morals to their stories. Whilst preparing this chapter I was watching a TV programme showing one of the very first films ever made. The storyline was simple. The heroine was a girl with some kind of disfigurement. All the boys ignored her. She was never invited to dances. But one day she met a blind man and they fell in love. Then came the remarkable news that he could be cured. There was, however, a drawback – it was going to cost money. Yes, you've guessed it – the unsightly girl had savings, and after a struggle she handed them over for his treatment. When the bandages were removed and he could see, he still loved her. The story had a happy ending. Of course, this is just a fairy story, but the motivation behind it is exactly the kind of response God is looking for from us.

He is looking for that attitude which puts others first before ourselves. The girl in the film risked losing all that she had – not only her material possessions but also the man she loved. Making sure the blind man in our experience stays on the right road can cost time, money and effort, and at the end of it all he may give you no thanks. But God will curse those who leave him to fall into a ditch. Of course, the blindness I'm speaking about is not only physical. Multitudes live in spiritual blindness, without the light of Jesus. Those who pedal false doctrines and philosophies cause the blind to be led astray. Clearly, God has a deep concern for all who are without sight or light. Should we be any less concerned?

The scripture goes on to speak of foreigners, orphans and people who are grief-stricken. God is so angered by injustice towards these people that failure to uphold his word brings down his curse. How do we react? Is our answer that we don't know any underprivileged people? Surely that can't be true. Have you ever been in a shop, for example, when someone from a minority group is being given poor service? Did you do the British thing and mind your own business? Perhaps you boiled inside and did nothing. You could at least have asked if you could help. Then after they had gone, you might politely have called for someone in authority and very, very politely aired your feelings about the treatment they had received. Remaining silent is not a viable option for us Christians.

No one can possibly adopt every orphan or feed all the hungry; that is not what God is asking of us. But to have a care for those who are brought into our orbit by the Lord is something we can be open to. However, reaching out can be dangerous; you never quite know where God will take you. A certain set of circumstances brought four little girls of mixed race into the life of a friend of mine. After an uphill struggle with the authorities, and with much prayer and support from their church, she and her husband have managed to adopt them, doubling the size of their family in one go! God is wanting to use ordinary people, just like you and me, to redress the injustices we find all around us. We don't need to create a lot of dust looking for opportunities; we're simply required to have open hearts and to be willing to be used by the Lord. He will guide us every step of the way.

Read: Psalm 72; Matthew 25:35-46.

Consider and pray: Spend time listening to God. He is waiting to speak to you plainly about the underprivileged. He needs your attention, as he may not say what you expect or want to hear. Listening is risky but rewarding. Because of his love for all men, he will send you as his envoy and help you to turn knowledge into action. He may lead you to the underprivileged in your street or on the other side of the globe. He has promised to be with you always and to give you everything you need to meet the challenges and finish your task. Consciously give yourself afresh today to serve the Lord Jesus and his purpose for your life.

I mentioned the subject of false doctrines. You may in the past have held certain beliefs or been influenced by wrong teaching. It is not enough simply to have had a change of heart. You need clearly to repudiate these beliefs, breaking any hold they had over you. Nothing must cast a shadow between us and the Lord.

8
Morality and the family

"Cursed is the man who sleeps with his father's wife . . . with any animal . . . with his sister [or half-sister] . . . with his mother-in-law." Then all the people shall say, *"Amen!"*

Deuteronomy 27:20-23

The Bible paints a picture of a loving heavenly Father who is very definitely not a prude about sex. After all, he did invent it! He made it extremely pleasurable, but as with all other aspects of life, he does have a few instructions he wants us to follow in order to maximise our safety and enjoyment. It's really very simple. Sex is designed to be a wonderful intimacy, between one man and one woman, for life. Anything else falls short of the maker's intentions. This narrows the field of activity quite drastically for us as Christians.

Society recognises the wisdom of having laws which, in the main, reflect God's laws, even though it does not recognise him at all. Medical science is well aware of the distress which in-breeding has caused. All kinds of defects and deformities can result from such unions. The

Habsburgs, who ruled in Europe from the thirteenth century to the nineteenth, through intermarriage acquired such a deformity – or perhaps you might call it an exaggeration. In-breeding had made the jaw overlarge, to the point where eating was difficult and they dribbled uncontrollably. The affliction became known as the "Habsburg Jaw". God, the great physician, fully understood the laws which govern our bodies long before man began to grapple with them.

The horrors of venereal diseases have never caused man to turn back to the maker's instructions. He has instead sought scientific and medical answers. The whole terrible AIDS plague is being handled in the same way. Man will find an answer which, if possible, allows him to continue with his promiscuous practices. But breaking the divine laws will have an adverse effect. If we're determined to defy gravity and fly without the aid of an aeroplane, we could climb to the edge of a precipice and throw ourselves off. We have the freedom to do this, but the result would be predictable – death! Sexual practices which are abhorrent to God carry his curse, and just as surely death will follow – albeit spiritual death.

It would be ridiculous to believe that the people of God are either blameless in these areas or exempt from God's curse. The curses given to Israel have an application to the church today. It isn't only the dirty linen of society at large which is coming out into the open. The sin which has been hidden in the church is also coming to light. We have been rocked, shocked and horrified over recent years as the incest and abuses in some of our Christian families have been exposed for all to see: fathers who have been having sexual relationships with their daughters, and sometimes sons, over a period of years; mothers who have turned a blind eye to their situations, perhaps because they couldn't or wouldn't believe what was happening. Some, unbelievably, have condoned these acts because they released them from sexual responsibility.

I have been involved in helping Christians to repent of and receive forgiveness for committing sexual perversions of many different kinds. Incest, homosexuality, bestiality, group sex, wife- and husband-swapping – all these have been happening under the surface, often cloaked with the veneer of religion. Sometimes these practices run in families, the sins of the fathers being passed down through the generations. Jesus is the answer. The curse can be broken, and even these people can be set completely free.

When these things were uncovered in Old Testament times, death was the just punishment. Then, as ever, God was exposing the sin. Even today, whether or not we are found out, if we avoid owning the sin and throwing ourselves on God's grace for forgiveness we are still alienated from life in God. Unrepentance drives a wedge between us and the Lord, slowly poisoning our whole relationship with him. Surely separation from one's Redeemer is indeed death, albeit a living one. Nothing is too difficult for God to do, except to forgive the sins of someone who will not allow him to. I have actually heard bestiality defended in these words: "It's okay, just as long as you don't hurt the animals." All things are justified either by "It's not hurting anyone" or by "It really feels good." Both are totally self-centred concepts. The false notion is that if you don't actually hurt someone, you don't have to face any comeback or recriminations, and as long as it feels good it's acceptable. Neither plea will be allowable in the heavenly court.

Some would argue, "Things are different now that Jesus has come; laws and curses are of no consequence." Don't you believe it. He simply took the whole law, which was already beyond us, fulfilled it in every part and elevated it way out of sight. The consequences of unrepented disobedience remain. The act of adultery was sin under the old order, and that went against man's desire for fresh experiences of multiple sexual partners. The new standard which Jesus brought was far higher. He taught that if you imagined having sex with someone, in his eyes it was exactly the same as physically committing the sin. Islam's teaching is dramatically opposed to this, although many Muslims would disagree and some even deny it, but here the woman has to be comprehensively covered from top to toe. She and she alone causes men to lust after her; men are totally innocent and the woman always guilty.

Our sexual practices are extremely important to the Lord, and perversion carries a heavy curse clause because of that. Do not wait to be found out; bring your immorality, whether in thought or deed, out into the light of Jesus' love. Let his Holy Spirit blow through your thought-life, and receive repentance as a precious gift of God. We can't achieve forgiveness on our own, but we can be certain that he who is the giver of all good gifts will be only too willing to meet our needs. He will forgive us freely and lift from us the heavy burden of his just curse, if we humbly seek his face.

Read: Romans 1:18-32; Micah 7:18-20.

Consider and pray: God desires that we have a right sexual orientation. He never condemns, however; he only convicts. He is infinitely patient and gracious with those who are struggling to find him, and he understands our frailty. If you have sinned in any of these ways, come before the Lord and fully acknowledge your sin. Throw yourself on his mercy. Confess your failure to God, but

35

also to trusted leaders in your church or fellowship. Take care not to do this unwisely or in a way which may cause others to stumble. Make sure you are not alone with a counsellor on a one-to-one basis, in order to safeguard yourself and them.

9

Hatred and violence

"Cursed is the man who kills his neighbour secretly." Then all the people shall say, "Amen!" "Cursed is the man who accepts a bribe to kill an innocent person." Then all the people shall say, "Amen!" "Cursed is the man who does not uphold the words of this law by carrying them out." Then all the people shall say, "Amen!"

Deuteronomy 27:24-26

In this section of the Deuteronomy scripture God is speaking about murder and assassination. How up-to-date the Bible is, with its definition of secret killing and murder for money. The only way people can live with the guilt burden of God's curse upon them is to convince themselves that he has no power to touch their lives. These crimes are not likely to be regular occurrences for you and I, in our families and churches. Perhaps they only become relevant when we introduce a New Testament slant on them. Then we may well find ourselves in the hot seat. I have already pointed out that the law of the Old Testament was impossible to keep, and that the New Testament standards which Jesus gave us are doubly out of reach. In his sermon on the mount Jesus put anger against your brother on a par with murder (Matthew 5:21-22).

There is a fair amount of neighbour-bashing going on, in a variety of situations, amongst Christians today. Isn't blackening someone's character or speculation about another's motives like secret murder? So many stories circulate, often without any foundation in truth. Someone looks very sad, or tired, or fed up, or angry, and a whole tale can be woven from a mere look. People in the public eye, such as film stars, royalty and MPs, often suffer this particular assault.

Accusations passed on are like the Chinese whispering game. You whisper into the ear of the person next to you, and by the time it gets around the circle, the original phrase is unrecognisable. I remember a monologue that Bernard Miles used to perform which touched on the subject of speculation. I can't recall the exact wording, but it ended something like this: "Old Mrs Brown saw my barrow outside the Rose and Crown every evenin', Monday to Sunday. 'That's intemperance!' she said. 'That's intemperance!' So I parked my barrow outside 'er 'ouse. I left it there all night! That 'ad 'er!'" Because his barrow was outside the pub, or Mrs Brown's house, for that matter, it didn't follow that he had spent his time there. That kind of assumption is character assassination and is an example of what the New Testament is speaking about.

Verse 26 of Deuteronomy 27 adds a further sobering note. God curses those who don't uphold the words of these laws by carrying them out. Remember, God is not wanting to reveal truth to us in order to make us afraid or condemned, or so that we might ignore it. His desire is that we should enter into his blessing, come to understand and practise his purposes and trust him implicitly. At the end of this section, where we have been considering the effects of God's direct curses on our lives, let us take stock to see how and where we have failed. Let us ask him to make his will plain, so that through repentance and forgiveness we may enter into a new phase of holiness in our relationship with him.

Read: Matthew 5:21-26; Psalm 11:1-7; James 3:1-12.

Consider and pray: Are you guilty of backbiting and gossip? Have you, with slander, destroyed a person's character? Or have you failed to stop those who have poured their lies into your ears, making you a partaker of their sin? We will have no power to bring conviction of sin to others whilst these sins, and those referred to in the previous five meditations, are found in our midst. James tells us that the tongue is the most unruly member of our body; let us ask the Holy Spirit for his power to control it. Determine to reject gossipmongering as well as all other forms of hatred and violence.

10
Curses cross time

At that time Joshua pronounced this solemn oath: "Cursed before the Lord is the man who undertakes to rebuild this city, Jericho: At the cost of his firstborn son will he lay its foundations; at the cost of his youngest will he set up its gates."

Joshua 6:26

In Ahab's time, Heil of Bethel rebuilt Jericho. He laid its foundations at the cost of his firstborn son Abiram, and he set up its gates at the cost of his youngest son Segub, in accordance with the word of the Lord spoken by Joshua son of Nun.

1 Kings 16:34

"And now this admonition is for you, O priests . . ." says the Lord Almighty. "I will send a curse upon you . . . Because of you I will rebuke your descendants . . ."

Malachi 2:1-3

We need to understand and appreciate the durability of God's curses. It is clear that some are avoidable through obedience to God's will; the story of Jonah and the

Ninevites shows us this. Some other curses are our lot because of our family background; the descendants were cursed in this way. It is also true that some curses affect us every day of our lives simply because we are members of the fallen human race. An example of this we can read in Genesis 11. God looked down upon the earth and saw the pride and arrogance in men's hearts. In order to prevent us from destroying ourselves, in his mercy he struck us with confusion by dividing us into language groups. Thousands of years later, in our ignorance, we continue to be frustrated and troubled by this. God's words are indeed durable.

Man is able to curse on behalf of God, and such a curse may last through generations. God takes these things very seriously and expects us to do exactly the same. Between the events in the first two readings there is a time lapse of around 500 years. Joshua's words had lost none of their power. They had not been watered down over the years, because he spoke them from the heart of God.

There are three aspects involved in a curse: the proclamation, the effects and, in the case of a God-given curse as a result of sin, the punishment, which may have eternal consequences. The effects can be seen in our bodies and emotions and may also have repercussions in our families and even outside. In Christ, curses and punishments are dealt with through his death and resurrection for all who believe. However, we need to appropriate this victory in order to see the effects of the curses and punishments nullified in our day-to-day existence. What's more, God's curses remain unaltered unless we receive Christ's atoning sacrifice.

Let me explain a little further. Death is man's lot; everyone without exception is born to die. And yet the victory of Jesus makes all the difference for Christians.

Praise God! Because of this, even though we die in this life, we are destined to live for ever with him. Now supposing 99% of the population turned to Christ, that would not weaken the curse of death for the 1% left. It stands immovable. Exactly the same is true for our families. When God, in his mercy, frees an individual from a chain of events which may have started generations before, he doesn't deal with the entire family – only with those who seek his forgiveness. The law and order of God's decrees will always remain. We must never lose sight of the fact that sin doesn't become righteousness or a pardonable mistake with the passage of time. Sin stands forever.

For those who do repent and receive Jesus' forgiveness, the scars or effects of past curses often hang around in the form of weakness, disease, depression and so on. It is our task in the church to work together to see these things broken in a practical and visible sense. The victory is already ours in Christ, but Satan contests our receiving it in the here and now. Hence Jesus' call for us to pray, "Your kingdom come, your will be done *on earth* as it is in heaven."

John and I have an adopted daughter of mixed race origin. The short story is that I used to be a child-minder and foster mother and was asked to take this little girl as an emergency measure. Her natural parents left her with me one day and never returned. She was a battered baby. During the protracted adoption procedure we were warned time and time again by our social worker, "You must remember for the future that battered babies batter their babies." This indeed is an admission, albeit from a non-Christian, that curses pass down through the generations. This lady sincerely believed that there was a very slim chance of our daughter being able to break the mould. She had, of course, no knowledge of Jesus, and although I told her about the Lord, without faith it was impossible for her to believe that things could change.

Our daughter had a relationship with the Lord, and while at this present time she isn't interested in spiritual things, he did break the effects of this curse in her life. She has a lovely little daughter, who has not been battered. The world recognises that these things happen, without any understanding of their origins. They talk freely about traits, recurring events and things running in families. We have heard from our parents and grandparents over and over again such phrases as "Like father, like son" and "Blood will out, you know!"

How is it that we, the people of God, so often refuse to take these things seriously? How is it that we wear blinkers which restrict our vision? We are constantly saying to God, "Bless me here, bless me there, bless me, bless me," whilst completely ignoring the historic bondages which prevent the blessing of God from flowing in our lives. We are desperate for blessing but forget God's other laws. He will not allow us to flout them, nor will he overlook them out of sentiment.

There are, then, certain practices which are expressly forbidden by God. Jesus himself made it clear that he came not to do away with the law, but to fulfil it. Our part is, with the Holy Spirit's help, to identify these areas and allow the sacrifice of Jesus to become effective in them, so that generations of wrongdoing are wiped out. Once this transformation has happened, we need to live our lives in the light of this freedom. However, many things which we find in our natural family tree and which are still affecting us today, were actually placed there by God, either directly or by him working through men. God has done this for our good. It does seem strange that curses can be placed there for our benefit, but it's true. We consider the word "curse" to be always negative. Could it not also be a positive thing, a signpost leading us into God's presence? This must surely be a good outcome.

Reading the Bible with eyes which appreciate that God has our best interests at heart will undoubtedly open our understanding to his statutes. Psalm 119 says it so well: "It was good for me to be afflicted so that I might learn your decrees." I am filled with admiration for David, who wrote these words. He indeed seems to have grasped and embraced the truth that God knows what he is doing, all of the time. We too can achieve this intimate relationship with and knowledge of God.

Read: Genesis 11:1-9; Psalm 119:65-80.

Consider and pray: Perhaps there are certain ungodly traits, occurrences or diseases which you see running through your family. God wants you to be free from all of these hindrances. The Holy Spirit is well able to pinpoint the area of a curse as we seek his guidance. Such things as a bad temper, compulsions of all kinds, miscarriage, divorce, failing eyesight, deafness, skin disorders, premature deaths and many, many more, *may* all be there as a result of a curse given even years before. It may be helpful to pray the prayer Jesus gave us: "Lead us not into temptation and deliver us from evil." Also be prepared to ask for help from those in your church who have some understanding of historic bondages of this sort. Remember too that not all our problems can be traced back to such curses.

11
Evil for good

"Love your enemies, do good to those who hate you, bless those who curse you, pray for those who mistreat you."

Luke 6:27-28

If a man pays back evil for good, evil will never leave his house.

Proverbs 17:13

As Christians we are familiar with the idea of repaying evil with good. However, in reality it is all too often the reverse. In the Old Testament even David repaid good with evil on one occasion. Uriah was a dedicated soldier. David had his allegiance and his trust, and yet he killed him. David had committed adultery with Bathsheba, and in his effort to cover up his sin he murdered Uriah her husband by sending him into a suicide situation in battle. God judged David harshly for this terrible deed, and his son by Bathsheba died. We may not send people into battle to die, but nevertheless trust is being violated every day in relationships between Christians. We repay good with evil, so we are just as guilty as David.

What about the husband who after many years of good marriage convinces himself that it would be best for everyone concerned if he were to leave his family, so that they could all have a fresh start? Actually, it's himself he's thinking about. His wife is no longer young, or slim, or she doesn't have quite the right image for his job. Then there is the woman who totally rejects her mother, although her mother loves her and cares for her. Her feelings of loathing are so strong that she cannot bear to be told how like her mother she is. I guess we've all come across social climbers who phase out trusted friends simply because they consider the relationships to be no longer appropriate to their new status. And then there are those of a different race or denomination to ourselves who have held out the hand of friendship but, because of our prejudice, have been turned away. And then there is the member of the family who became overweight or who was mentally or physically retarded, whose greatest fault was that they enjoyed being with us; but they were unlovely, so they were excluded and ignored. All of these and many, many more are day-to-day examples that I have come across in counselling situations. Returning evil for good is commonplace amongst Christians as well as in the world.

The New Testament also warns us about the practice. For example, the disciples were instructed by Jesus that when they entered a town to bring the good news, they were to look for a worthy person and stay in their home. If they were well received they were to let their peace rest there. If they were treated badly, or in other words received evil for their good, they were to leave that place, shaking the dust from their feet and taking with them their peace or blessing. The Lord went on to say that it will be better for Sodom and Gomorrah on the day of judgment than for such a place, which rejects his messengers and therefore his salvation by returning evil for good. During a visit to India, I was able to put Jesus' advice into action.

I had the privilege of taking part in village meetings to which not only Christians, but also Animists, Hindus and Muslims came to hear the word of God. Afterwards we were offered hospitality and a place to sleep for the night in some homes, which although not Christian, were worthy and welcoming. Many of them were just one step from the kingdom. John and I prayed for God's blessing to come to such houses. In fact, we later returned to the area and found that in one small village between forty and sixty of those people had come to Christ after our travelling companion, Ian Farr, had preached the gospel. Again we were cared for in a home which up to that evening had been Hindu. So, it is not as much our belief which hinders God, as our attitude. Whatever our belief, rejection of God's word and his messengers is repaying evil for good. But there are many other ways in which we do this both in society and in the church.

The whole attitude of dog eat dog – that is, if you don't tread on someone to get ahead, that person will surely tread on you – is rampant amongst leaders in business and politics. Deep and long-standing working relationships are terminated overnight. Such words as love, trust and friendship have been debased until they have almost no meaning. Judas is an outstanding example of returning evil for good in an effort to get ahead. At the last supper, Jesus called him a friend and told him to go and do what he had to do. The Lord was the perfect companion, the most gracious leader, the finest teacher; but in spite of all this, Judas betrayed and rejected him.

Leaders in the church are quite often victims of rejection, and they have their clay feet. They had them from the beginning, when they were helping us with all the problems in our lives, but suddenly, if they ask something of us by way of commitment or giving, we really don't like it. The good they did is forgotten and all we can see is their weaknesses. We label them hard or judgmental or misguided, and leave that church, moving on somewhere else. Once we start moving on for this kind of reason it becomes a habit, or we give up fellowship altogether and do nothing. Once again we are guilty of returning evil for good. Peace has left our houses and lives and unrest is here to stay.

This exchange of evil for good consistently happens in government – in local councils, district councils, national governments and international bodies. Statements of intent are rescinded, at times without any explanation. Agreements and treaties which have been ratified are frequently broken. Most nations have plenty of examples of such injustice in their histories. In the case of the USA, for instance, there is the treatment which the Red Indians received.

We British have more than our fair share; our past is littered with broken promises. For instance, the war between Britain and China in the second half of the nineteenth century was based on our desire to balance our budget sheets. The Chinese gave us trading rights, which was good, but they banned the import of opium, as they wanted to stop addiction amongst their people. Illegally we flooded China with the drug, causing untold misery to thousands; that was evil. God is deeply concerned with national exchanges of evil for good. They will be judged, as we read in Matthew 25.

Evil for good

Evil is doing that which God judges to be unacceptable. We all tend to consider our own consciences to be the plumbline between right and wrong. However, every one of us is twisted in one way or another. Some have tender consciences and others have tough ones. Either may have been distorted through hurts and hang-ups and even biased Bible teaching. Only the Holy Spirit can instruct us. He will take the scales from our eyes and if needs be discipline us in order that we come to understand what God's expectations are. Our cultural as well as our Christian programming has dulled our consciences, and therefore our behaviour has been affected. In the light of this we need to re-evaluate our understanding of how the Lord measures good and evil. We must ensure that our practice is in tune with his word and that we are not responsible for dealing out evil for good.

Read: Matthew 7:7-12 & 25:31-46.

Consider and pray: Meditate for a while on this whole matter of returning evil for good. Think back over your past relationships. Have you marginalised friends or relatives? Have you allowed pride, jealousy or ambition to cause you to repay kindness with rejection? I'm not suggesting that you frantically dig around to find things. Be still, and the Lord will speak to you if you really mean business with him. He only wants to do you good, even when it means pain during the process. Now receive his freedom and forgiveness, and don't be afraid to take steps to put things right with any concerned, if you are able. Revivals have been known to start in this way!

12

Direct satanic influence

His wife said to him, "Are you still holding on to your integrity? Curse God and die!" He replied, "You are talking like a foolish woman. Shall we accept good from God, and not trouble?"

Job 2:9-10

We learn from the story of Job that Satan is directly and intimately involved in bringing mankind to the place where we curse God and die. The devil has his demonic forces, ready to do his bidding in an endeavour to lead us into temptation. The Lord also has his angelic hosts. This, however, is where the comparison ends. These two forces are not of equal strength. No one, not even Lucifer himself, has the ability to see all, to be everywhere and to know all thoughts; these attributes are the preserve of God alone. The Bible teaches us that as Christians we have a far greater power residing within us than the evil destructive power which is at large in the earth. Having said this, Satan and his minions are a force to be reckoned with and we need to be alert.

We see Satan's terrible hand at work throughout the scriptures, and world history is full of the horrendous deeds he has inspired. To say that we are totally immune to his interference is actually to believe that we have arrived at perfection. This enemy of ours uses any available means, structure or organisation as his vehicle. In Bible times he demonised ordinary people; we have the accounts. He manipulated men in high office, such as Herod. He used even the Jewish religious leaders, whom Jesus scathingly described as being "of their father the devil". And on one occasion at least Satan worked through Peter, one of Jesus' closest followers. Sorcerers, fortune-tellers, witches and mediums are also his co-workers, seeking to gain ascendency over men's souls. Nothing has changed; they are still used by him to peddle his pollution. Reading your horoscope once may not do you any obvious harm, but it can be the thin edge of a very fat wedge, leading you into a dependency. Some people can't start their day without knowing what the stars have in store for them. Ronald Reagan's wife, Nancy, is said to be such a person, relying on this so-called guidance.

In May 1990 I was at a Christian Bible event. I had been asked to go to one particular session in the children's programme. It was for those aged seven to eleven. The team wanted me there as part of the back-up whilst the workers tackled the subject of the occult. At the close of the meeting there was an appeal, and the children flocked forward. We were extremely busy for quite a while. The group allocated to me had been suffering from nightmares on a fairly regular basis. We prayed and talked and slowly a sad picture emerged. These children, mostly from Christian families, came from a variety of schools and denominational backgrounds. In spite of this, most had fallen into the trap which the enemy had set. Horoscopes in comics, breakfast TV with astrologers like Russell Grant, tarot cards and ouija boards at school and in clubs, had all been involved. Seeing these children set free, with sensitivity and a great deal of love, with much prayer and no fuss and bother, was a great privilege. Imagine adding to these young lives years of habit-forming superstition, and you get a glimpse of the problem which exists amongst adults. It is the responsibility of all of us to take every opportunity to combat these influences.

When accosted by the gypsy in the market-place, offering lucky white heather or to tell your fortune, what do you do? She may threaten you verbally, cursing you with bad luck, or giving you a black look, muttering things under her breath about your future. The Bible recommends blessing for cursing and turning the other cheek. Taking no action is not an option. Satan delights in passive saints who turn in on themselves, living in fear lest the gypsy's curse might be effective. This is the kind of ground Satan loves to take. How about rounding on the gypsy and soundly telling her off? Well, that's better than nothing! At least your action would give God an opportunity, either to speak to the gypsy or to tell you how dumb you've been. Then we can put things right with the Lord and learn from our mistake, leaving nothing for the enemy to work on. Of course, it is better to find a way to bless and turn the other cheek. This may mean offering to buy a hotdog or a cup of tea and a sandwich. It may mean spending some time chatting and praying. In my experience the standard answer to such a suggestion has been a large amount of spit narrowly missing my foot, but don't let this kind of response put you off.

In all this the Lord is looking for people who are aware of Satan's activities and where he is likely to turn up, without being paranoid or afraid. Our task is, in peace and confidence, to listen for God's directives, to oust the dark powers and to be available to those seeking release. No saint is exempt from playing his or her part in exposing the enemy's attempts to infiltrate our families and churches. We need to work together, supporting and encouraging one another.

Read: Job 1:6-22 & 2:1-10; Acts 16:16-18.

Consider and pray: Has there been some demonic influence in your life which has made you afraid? No matter how minimal you feel this is, bring it before the Lord. Superstition, occult practice, horoscopes, tea leaves, palmistry – if there has been anything which may have let our enemy in, bring it out into God's light and confess it before him. Even if you have not dabbled, fear of or preoccupation with the supernatural should be dealt with. Ask another Christian to pray with you. It should be someone sympathetic and experienced in these things, and preferably someone known in your church. They can pray for deliverance if it is needed and speak blessing into those areas which concern you. God is waiting to exchange cursing for blessing.

13

Appointed to bear fruit

In the morning, as they went along, they saw the fig tree withered from the roots. Peter remembered and said to Jesus, "Rabbi, look! The fig-tree you cursed has withered."

Mark 11:20

The account of the cursing of the fig tree is in two parts which occur either side of Jesus dealing with the money-changers in the temple. At first, to us it seems rather a strange story, when we think of the Lord cursing a fig tree. Later, as Jesus and his disciples pass by once more, Peter calls our attention to it again. This tree was obviously on their route from Jerusalem to Bethany and would be a constant reminder to them all of Jesus' words and actions. Why did Jesus curse the figtree in this way? What did it have to do with the temple? And how must we apply this to ourselves?

Horticulturalists would tell us that although it wasn't actually the season for figs, if there were leaves on the tree, there should also have been some fruit. The fruit of this particular tree appeared before the leaves. Even so, poor little tree, it does seem harsh that it should be so blighted by the Lord. His words were final. It wasn't simply that the tree would never bear fruit again; Jesus went further than that, and the figtree died from the root up. This meant that the leaves would stay green for a short time, as the sap in the branches continued to nourish them.

We need to understand the symbolism Jesus is using here, and the lesson of faith and fruitfulness he is teaching his disciples. This story would have been retold many times. The fig tree would have been looked at and marvelled over by travellers on that same road. Jesus had just experienced his triumphant entry into Jerusalem, with the crowds laying down their garments and branches from the trees as a pathway for him. This was the equivalent in their own culture of our red carpet treatment. He went on to the temple and looked around. He then left the city, passing the fig tree on his way to Bethany, where his friends Mary, Martha and Lazarus lived. There must have been a singing, rejoicing crowd still lingering with Jesus and the disciples. No one goes home willingly after such an extra-special party as they had all had on this, the first Palm Sunday. The people greeted Jesus like a king, but he knew that this effusive reception was only skin deep. These same people would soon be shouting for his blood.

Through the fig tree, Jesus was actually making a judgment on the temple, its priests and the worshippers. There was plenty of show in the temple – lots of activity and public praying, with sacrifices being bought and sold. All had an appearance of godliness, but Jesus found no fruit to satisfy his Spirit. There was no faith. He actually called it a "den of robbers", and turning his back on the scene, looked for fellowship elsewhere. Later he prophesied (see Mark 13) that not one stone of that temple would be left on another. As he had cursed the fig tree, and it withered from the root upwards, so also he cursed the temple. Yes, the show did go on for another seventy years, but it was already dead at the root and was finally totally demolished.

We are now God's living temple, and he is looking for the fruit of faith in our lives. Jesus' curse still applies today. If we are found to be all show and no substance, we will not be a blessing to the Lord. Jesus is not looking for activity, a great bustle and stir – in other words, lots of leaves. Leaves are fine, even necessary, but he wants to part them and find the fruits of our faith – love, joy, peace, patience, kindness, goodness, faithfulness, gentleness and self control – nestling there in the branches of our lives and churches. He may, at times, prune our leaves and branches back, in order that our strength will be used in more fruit-bearing, rather than in producing a massive leafy show.

Just as Jesus warned the complacent churches of Revelation that he would remove their candlesticks or spit them out of his mouth, so lukewarm Christians today must face his judgment. He looks for enjoyment from his fig tree, and he wants it to nourish and sustain the weary traveller. Our praise and sacrifice must go beyond words and duty, and should come from hearts which overflow with love towards God and his world. Such faith can move the mountains of formalism and produce fruit-filled saints and churches.

Read: Mark 11:12-21; Romans 7:4-6; Revelation 2:1-7 & 3:14-22.

Consider and pray: Is your life so full of activity that you are missing out on a heart-relationship with the Lord? Have you lost the warmth and enthusiasm of your first love? Perhaps you look back over your Christian life and realise that there has been little fruit at all, as you have been absorbed with the externals of your religion. Now is the time to take serious action and humble yourself before the Lord, seeking his forgiveness and restoration. The Holy Spirit is longing and waiting to receive you and meet your need, no matter how far you may have strayed into formalism and hypocrisy.

14

No room for curses

Like a fluttering sparrow or a darting swallow, an undeserved curse does not come to rest.

Proverbs 26:2

What an evocative verse this is. Solomon paints such a descriptive picture of the enemy with these few words. Anyone who has watched these birds searching for food in the garden or collecting building materials for their nests knows their fluttering and darting motions well. They do not stay very long in one place. Even if you have a bird table or bath, they rarely hang around. It's a quick swoop in and a faster retreat to a safer place. They watch and wait for the tempting morsel, the undefended water, the juicy worm. What a mode of operation. There is little time for rest. How different to an eagle or hawk, which bides its time and rarely misses its prey.

What is the Bible saying to us here? It is saying very clearly that where there is no landing place, no welcome, nothing to feed on, a curse cannot come to rest. This is indeed wonderful news. It is impossible for a curse to affect us if we are living our lives honestly before God, open to his word, his Son and his Spirit. By the same token, if we discover that a curse has been effective in our lives, this is no cause to panic. Admitting the truth doesn't make things worse with God, but may well bring about positive repercussions for us, as we work through all the implications. Let me give you an example.

At the end of a meeting a young man called Bob came and asked if he could speak to me. We sat down together at the back of the hall with another young man, Paul, who had introduced Bob to the Lord a few months previously. Bob told me how much Jesus was coming to mean to him and how his life had been revolutionised after he had been filled with the Holy Spirit. There was just one ongoing problem. For some years Bob had found it very difficult to sleep. He napped, but rarely slept through a night, and was subsequently always tired. What did I think? A verse of scripture came strongly to my mind: "for he grants sleep to those he loves" (Psalm 127:2).

Perhaps there was something here that God wanted me to use to bring Bob into blessing. We prayed and talked around the subject. Suddenly Bob said, "Oh, by the way, I've been meaning to ask what I should do with all the stuff." "Stuff?" I said, gloriously ignorant of what he was referring to. "Yes, I was a thief, and my flat is full of stuff I've nicked." You could have knocked me down with a feather. Obviously, there were bound to be repercussions as a result of this confession, but Paul and his church were committed to Bob. They helped him through the process of contacting the police and turning in all the stolen goods. He slept well from that night onwards.

Pretending there is no ground or covering ground up will not fool God or the devil. Trial by ordeal, exercised throughout the world, particularly during the Middle

Ages, was a reversal of the biblical model. In those times an innocent person had to survive terrible tortures to prove their innocence, whereas scripture prescribed a harmless test to establish guilt. This practice stemmed originally from the Jewish people. In Israel, if you feared that your partner had been unfaithful to you but had no proof, and because of your suspicions you were constantly plagued by jealousy, there was something you could do. You could go to the priest, who would sprinkle some dust from the floor of the tabernacle into water. Your partner would then stand before the Lord and drink this mixture. If guilty, they developed a wasting disease as the result of God's curse through the water. If they remained healthy they were innocent. The innocent had nothing to fear, the guilty everything. In this age of God's grace, how important it is to live in the innocence which is ours in Christ.

However, we do need to protect ourselves in the best way possible by wearing our spiritual armour. "Above all," Paul says, "take the shield of faith with which we can quench all the fiery darts" (Ephesians 6:16). The shield of faith is the weapon which enables us to combat fear and doubt. Fiery darts sting and burn, and they leave septic and painful wounds. They should not be allowed to land under any circumstances. The shield of faith is our extra protection against them. If we are equipped, Satan's curses and fiery darts, like fluttering birds, will find no resting place. The same principle holds good for all other kinds of curses, whether they come from witches, gypsies, witch-doctors or clairvoyants. There is nothing to fear, unless there is ground in your life on which they can land. If pins are stuck into a doll made in your likeness, they can cause you no pain, unless you fear that they can – that is the ground. With faith in Christ, we have no reason whatever to be afraid. In him we are more than conquerors.

Read: Ephesians 6:10-18; Psalm 91; Romans 8:31-39.

Consider and pray: What are the landing places and the toeholds the enemy has in our lives? Where is he able to trip us up and defeat us again and again? In peace and quietness come before the Lord without reproach. Identify the landing places and with God's help claim the ground back from Satan. Superstitions, habits, appetites, fears, temper, greed, dishonesty, religiosity and a thousand other weaknesses and sins provide the territory Satan needs to control us. We cease to be vulnerable when we are fully protected with God's armour and are walking in righteousness and faith.

15
Cursing for a purpose

"Now the hand of the Lord is against you. You are going to be blind, and for a time you will be unable to see the light of the sun."

Acts 13:11

Throughout the Bible, men and women of God curse other people or nations on God's behalf and at his prompting. We might say that since the Old Testament incidents were before the death of Jesus, we can spiritualise them away. We might well question and debate the whole concept of cursing people, in the light of Jesus' teaching that we should, when ill-used, turn the other cheek. However, we do have some New Testament instances – for example, the one in our Acts 13 scripture, which involved Paul and a magician called Elymas. This particular curse had a time limit on it, and was specifically brought to prevent the magician from interfering in the dialogue between his master, the proconsul Sergius Paulus, and Paul. This demonstration of God's power was so arresting that the proconsul immediately became a believer.

It cannot be stressed enough that we can only curse, under the anointing of the Spirit, those whom he leads us to. This is not a tool for evangelism which can be used willy-nilly. But how effective it would be if, by the Holy Spirit, you were to discern who was causing the interference in a person's life, keeping them from responding to the Lord. Then, with this knowledge, you would take action, cursing that person with dumbness or sleep or indeed with anything else the Spirit prompted. It would certainly have a startling effect, and I can think of many situations, particularly in reaching the unreached, where such evidence of God's presence could be extremely important.

Of course, this is not an isolated case. Again in Acts 23 Paul curses Ananias, the high priest. Here he promises death. His actual words are, "God will strike you, you whitewashed wall!" True, he went on to apologise, because he hadn't realised who he was cursing, but he did not retract the curse itself. "Well," you may say, "that's a safe one. Everyone is bound to die, sooner or later." In fact, Ananias died five years later – he was assassinated! You couldn't by any stretch of the imagination call that dying of natural causes in the passage of time! It was the fulfilment of Paul's words.

Peter, in Acts 5, cursed Sapphira. Her husband, another Ananias, came before Peter and lied about the amount of money he was giving. With a word of knowledge Peter uncovered the truth, and when Ananias heard it he immediately fell down dead and was carried out of the room. Later, Sapphira entered, unaware of what had happened, and Peter warned her that her fate would be the same as that of her husband. The men returning from carrying him out would carry her out also. Her death from his word was instantaneous. I'm sure the effect on the church was electric and must have caused the level of holiness to rise abruptly. Again, in chapter 8 of Acts, Peter cursed Simon the sorcerer, who thought he could buy the power of God with money. "May your money perish with you," Peter cried and called him to repent. Simon answered, "Pray to the Lord for me so that nothing you have said will happen to me."

Paul's instructions to the Corinthians concerning a man who persistently practised incest amount to cursing him, in my view. The apostle urged them to follow the Old Testament practice as far as sexual immorality was concerned. The man was to be put out of the church and his body was delivered to Satan for destruction, so that his soul might be saved. It does appear later that this course of action led to his repentance. It is indeed a heavy curse to be cut off from the congregation of those you love and to be forbidden to break bread. Unfortunately, we today are all too often unable to bring this kind of discipline to bear in our churches. If a person is put out of a fellowship, they can usually just pop down the road to another church, no questions asked. Frequently the same lesson has to be learned all over again.

Jesus also used curses on occasion. I have already mentioned the fig tree and also the curse he placed on the temple, which had such devastating effects. In Luke 10 we read that Jesus cursed the towns which rejected his mighty works and those of his disciples. To reject Jesus or his followers was to reject the one who had sent him, and this carried very serious consequences. In the following chapter a whole generation were condemned and held responsible for their hypocrisy and their treatment of the prophets. Jesus pulled no punches and left no one in any doubt as to their fate if they failed to acknowledge the work of God's Holy Spirit in himself or his chosen ones. As a result of watering down the message we see very little depth of conviction or fear of the Lord in our churches or evangelism.

Curses are not flashes of God's temper. In both the Old and New Testaments they are used as salutary lessons, through which the Lord seeks to communicate his ways to men. I would not anticipate that this practice of cursing would be an everyday occurrence, but we should be open to the Lord showing his power in this way. Examples of cursing have also been recorded in times of revival, bringing whole communities face to face with the reality of God's truth. After all, it's not only God's love which is the same yesterday, today and for ever, but also his judgment.

Read: Acts 5:1-11 & 13:6-12; Luke 10:8-16 & 11:47-51.

Consider and pray: The thought of cursing someone or something with a view to bringing them face to face with God's truth or presence is so alien to most Christians that they are closed to the whole concept. Let us pray for light on this matter in order to bring a sense of the fear of the Lord into our personal lives, our churches and our mission. Obviously, we must not work outside of the framework and covering of our church and its leadership, but we must expect God's supernatural powers to be manifest. Situations in our communities, in local government and in the business world must give way to the gospel of the kingdom and the power of the age to come. This will mean a deeper revelation of God's love and judgment!

PART II
BLESSINGS

16
From cursing into blessing!

Our God, however, turned the curse into a blessing.

Nehemiah 13:2

The book of Nehemiah is all about putting the city of Jerusalem back into order. At great cost and with care and patience the walls were rebuilt and the gates were hung. The Ammonites and Moabites could not be included in the assembly of God. The historical reasons for this were read aloud for all the people to hear from the law of Moses. These nations had not helped Israel with food and water in their time of need, and had actually hired Balaam to curse them. But try as he might he could not do it. Every time he stood to curse, out came a blessing. Nehemiah looked back and declared, "Our God, however, turned the curse into a blessing." We also look back, but to Jesus, who redeemed us from the curse of the law by becoming a curse for us. As it is written in Galatians 3:13, "Cursed is everyone who is hung on a tree."

After our failure in the garden, God began preparing a way back to himself for us. Immediately he instituted the patriarchal order as an authority structure and holding operation, until the appointed time for his Son to be born. We were, indeed, cursed in Genesis as a result of our folly. The law was imposed upon us. It would continually uncover our wickedness, as God knew we would be unable to keep it. With the coming of Jesus the law was fulfilled, our bills were all paid up, the old man was nailed to the cross and a new humanity was born. Through rebirth in the Saviour our God did it again – he turned the curse into blessing.

Jesus was not just cursed by God at Calvary, which would have been terrible enough, but he actually became a curse for us. Oh yes, the religious people of his day clearly wanted him hung on that cross. They knew the scriptures and were looking for overwhelming evidence that his claim to be the Son of God was false. If Jesus was hung on the tree, it would prove beyond doubt that he was cursed by God, and this would litigate against him. These wicked men understood well the requirements of the law. Because they refused to believe that he was the Messiah, they applied the law to establish that it was impossible for him to be the Redeemer for whom they had waited for so long. However, in their blind fury they had completely missed God's heart and had failed to understand the transaction which was about to take place through that sacrificial death.

In all cases of misdemeanour, the law requires a judgment – innocent or guilty? The judgment demands a sentence – freedom or death? When the law is broken, there has to be a presence in the dock. As the law-breakers, humanity became the accused. We are guilty and stand condemned; we cannot keep God's law. We are sinners, and therefore we will never make it on our own. Of course, God understands the terrible circumstances which many have endured and the ways in which we have been sinned against, but we cannot offer these as an excuse or reason for our own sins. He will deal kindly with us when we repent, but until then our end is predictable and inevitable. Mitigating circumstances are of no consequence. The fact that we didn't have a good start in life – that we were adopted or abused, or were born not very bright – does not mean that we can't be held accountable for our actions. Each one of us is responsible, and the only way out is for someone perfect to take our place in the dock.

This is exactly what Jesus has done for us. Furthermore, he didn't only take my sin upon himself, he actually *became* sin for me, carrying it into the grave and burying it there for ever. I shall never fully understand how he could bear to do such a thing, but I know that he did. Caiaphas the high priest and his cohorts had not taken into account the reality that the law would work against them and for Jesus, because of his perfection. As high priest, he was the one man above all others who should have grasped the secret knowledge of God's mercy and judgment, hidden there in the statutes. But as always, "God opposes the proud, but gives grace to the humble" (James 4:6).

The cross obliterated everything that could possibly stand between us and God's blessing. Just as the veil was torn in the temple, opening the way for all men into the holy of holies, so, supernaturally, the darkness was pierced, allowing the light of God's amazing love to break through and deliver us from all the powers of death and hell.

Read: Galatians 3:10-14; Isaiah 53:1-12.

Consider and pray: Whatever stands between us and the blessing of God has been removed! Jesus has already done it; are we willing to receive? We who have been born of the

Spirit are now joint heirs with Christ. The whole of the Bible and its promises are ours. By faith Abraham is our father and Christ is our Friend and Saviour. The Holy Spirit has been poured out so that we can share Jesus' work on the cross. Amen! Praise and worship God, thanking him for all that is yours through Jesus Christ. Begin to actively reach out for more of the blessings which he has reserved for you and is longing to give you.

17
Our father Abraham

"I will make you into a great nation and I will bless you; I will make your name great, and you will be a blessing. I will bless those who bless you, and whoever curses you I will curse; and all the peoples on earth will be blessed through you."

Genesis 12:2-3

What great and wonderful promises God made to Abraham, and many generations later he is still fulfilling them. When we read the stories of the heroes and heroines of the Bible, we sometimes forget that they didn't know the end of their own stories. What we read in a few moments represents years of a life, with all its struggles and pain. We see things panoramically, from beginning to end, and because of this are inclined to dehumanise these men and women. We are always in danger of trivialising their agony of choice and times of decision, or of putting them on pedestals remote from our own efforts to serve and love the Lord. As Christians we are recipients of these great blessings through the centuries. Because we walk by faith we too have become sons and daughters of Abraham. He and his wife Sarah were human, just as we are. They had to grow towards the Lord and come to the place where he called them his friends. By their walk they cleared a path of faith for us to tread, and so we share their blessings.

The story of Abraham actually begins with his father, Terah. He took his family and set out to go to Canaan, but he settled in Haran and died there. Many things must have happened to Terah whilst he was in Haran, and they were evidently enough to prevent him from finishing his journey to Canaan. Later, God instructed Abraham to complete the course started by his father. Both father and son were God-fearing men; one settled and the other went on into the blessings of God.

There is so much to be learned from Abraham and Sarah, and it isn't all success by a long chalk. In Egypt they lied about their marriage, causing Sarah to become Pharaoh's wife. Then their herdsmen fought with the herdsmen of Lot, Abraham's nephew, and they agreed to separate. God promised them a son, but despite this Sarah encouraged Abraham to sleep with her maid Hagar, and then complained about Hagar's attitude towards her once she became pregnant. With Abraham's support she ill-treated Hagar, forcing her to run away.

Barring cultural differences, their struggles were much the sort of thing you and I face day by day in our walk with God. The temptation to be deceptive, trouble between workers, family relationship problems, wrong attitudes towards people – these things are just as real to us today. It is truly amazing how much Abraham and Sarah messed things up, but God continued to work with them and finally blessed them. He knew their frailty, but he also knew that their hearts were towards him as they travelled on in obedience, not settling for less than God's very best. I trust that we too are learning from our mistakes and refusing to accept a good life as a substitute for the fullness which God has promised to all who press on towards the goal.

So the story of Abraham and Sarah is full of promises and contradictions. They were to found a nation, but when they died they had only one son. They were to occupy a land, but all they ever possessed was a burial plot. They were looking for a city, but owned only a tent, constantly moving from one place to another. Yet God's promises to them were true. From these two sprang the whole teeming nation of Israel, as numerous as grains of sand on the seashore. And still the promises of God continue, for now the church has been born. Its members are like countless shining stars filling the heavens. Truly, in Abraham all the nations of the earth are blessed, and we, although not Israelites by natural birth and circumcision, are Abraham's children by faith, and so heirs to God's promises.

Abraham died without seeing, with his physical eyes, the full outworking of God's word, which is still reaching its fulfilment in us. With him, and with those yet to come, we travel to that city of peace, the New Jerusalem. By faith, as God's new people of promise, the church of Jesus Christ is journeying towards the fullness of the kingdom of God. Right now we are becoming partakers of its future blessings; we are receiving a foretaste of what is yet to come!

Read: Hebrews 11:8-19; Revelation 21:1-7.

Consider and pray: Meditate on your roots; they go back beyond Jesus to Abraham, who looked for him. See yourself as a part of God's history and plan for creation from the very beginning of time. You too are a chosen vessel. You are called to receive God's love by faith in Christ and to be a partaker of all the blessings which God purposed to pass on to his people, even before time began. Now, take your place alongside those who have gone before and live under those blessings which he has reserved for his people.

18
The promised land of blessing

*"The Lord your God will drive out those nations before you,
little by little. You will not be allowed to eliminate them all at
once, or the wild animals will multiply around you."*

Deuteronomy 7:22

God never promised that following him would be a bed of
roses. In Deuteronomy 20, his battle instructions com-
menced with the words, "When you go to war against your
enemies . . ." – not "If . . ." Spiritual warfare will continue to be part and parcel of our experience until Jesus
comes back. When called to enter the promised land, the
Israelites could not face the battle involved the first time
around. Only Caleb and Joshua saw things with God's
eyes – the eyes of faith. After viewing the land, they
reported that it was full of "milk, honey and grapes the
size of footballs. Oh, by the way, there were a few giants,
but nothing really to worry about." The other spies whom
Moses sent saw something quite different: "Giants – lots
of giants, huge and threatening! Giants that will crush us
like grasshoppers. And, oh yes, it's true the land did seem

to be fairly fertile." Today it is a similar story. We Christians can view things through the eyes of faith or of unbelief.

I reckon that I could have built a house if I'd received a brick every time I heard someone say, "My troubles didn't start until I became a Christian." Well, isn't that the truth of the matter? What else should we expect? After all, we do have an enemy who is committed to keeping us from God's blessings. The wilderness may not have been a wonderful place, but we knew what to expect there. We learned to cope with things, or ignore them as the case might be. But giants — who needs them? Then we were in darkness, lost in our sin and blissfully ignorant of the facts. We didn't understand how dark it really was, just feeling from time to time that there must be more to life than we were experiencing. Then the light shone into our darkness. We began to see the way forward and to understand that God had prepared another place for us.

That was when we saw the giants. Suddenly they loomed large on our horizon. For example, we learned that our thought-life had to be conquered. Whereas before, we could fantasise about the girl at the office, or the man in the car saleroom at the top of the road. We could no longer do that any more. It seemed that we were being attacked on all sides, not only within but from without as well. Our husband is out of work; our wife is sick; the children are in trouble at school; there's the car accident, the rising mortgage rates, the larger-than-usual bills. The battle is on!

When David met his giant, Goliath cursed him. He scorned his youth and inexperience and said to him, "Come here! I'll give your flesh to the birds of the air and the beasts of the field!" David did not retreat, but with his seemingly inadequate weapons he brought that giant down. It wasn't his strength or skill, but his implicit trust in God's strategy that killed Goliath. In our weakness the Lord will be our strength and fight for us, just as he did for David. The whole Philistine army was routed that day; they fled not from a shepherd boy, but from the King of Kings and the Lord of Lords who stood beside him on the battlefield. Our giants must be dealt with if we are to enter and enjoy the promised land of God's blessing. It will not happen all at once – that would be too much for us – but little by little they will be driven out and defeated.

It was God's time for Jane. Premenstrual tension had dominated her existence for years, like an ogre bearing down on her and becoming larger all the time. The doctor had been unable to help. She had participated in group therapy, but that had only encouraged her to withdraw from pressure, leaving her life more and more restricted. Seeing that this condition ruled so many women's lives, she determined to do battle and seek God's help to break free. Together we prayed, and the curse was cancelled. "With God's help I'll never allow that to control me again!" she cried. You may feel that this was a physical liability about which Jane could do nothing, but she knew differently. For her it was a giant. For some considerable time now she has stood her ground and continued to enjoy her liberty. She is one of dozens of women I've seen win this same victory.

We will, no doubt, meet with setbacks and failures, but we do need to plug into God's strength in order to press on, gaining in experience and faith as we go. We may need time to consolidate what God has done for us, but with his help we can move on once more. After God dealt with enemies in my life, as I looked back I discovered that the giants were only cardboard cut-outs without any substance. Truly, as David discovered, even death is but a shadow as we walk on with God.

Often our problem is that, like ducks in a shooting gallery, our giants seem to keep popping up again all over the place.

Satan does not usually tempt us with new things, but plays on our weak spots in his attempts to bring us down. When we give in to his onslaughts, his troops appear to multiply like wild animals around us. So the Lord is gracious, and if we stay close to him, he does not allow us to be over-extended by fighting on many fronts at the same time. He knows that we just couldn't cope, so it's little by little, and he's with us every step of the way. Like the Israelites of old, the land is ours to be enjoyed and lived in. God desires to bless us with all that milk, honey and fruit, but we must press on past Jericho and take it all in Jesus' name.

Read: Deuteronomy 7:17-26; Numbers 13:21-33.

Consider and pray: You may have experienced wonderful crisis victories in your life, like Jericho's fall. But the Lord also wants you to face the process of pressing on with him day by day. Perhaps you have been looking for a "once and for all" end to your struggles with yourself and your circumstances. But the Lord wants to take you deeper with him in trust as you walk with him through the temptations and trials. Pray that the Lord will show you the reality of a steady walk with him, slowly increasing the pace. In this way you avoid the stop-start, go-back-to-the-beginning experience you have wrestled with in the past. You will mount up with wings as eagles, you'll run and not be weary!

19
Soldiers all!

"Most blessed of women be Jael, the wife of Heber the Kenite, most blessed of tent-dwelling women."

Judges 5:24

At first sight this may seem to be a strange passage to draw upon; perhaps it is difficult to relate to a modern-day setting. But Jael has much to commend her as a pattern for us to follow. This lady looked out of her tent, saw Sisera, the enemy, skulking along and enticed him into her dwelling, where she could deal with him. She lulled him into a false sense of security, giving him a drink of milk and a place to hide. When he nodded off, she took a tent peg and a mallet, hammering the peg right through his head. For this she was blessed by God.

We too may enter into the blessings of God through this woman's example of uncompromising aggression. But what is God communicating to us through her story? Firstly, Jael was an ordinary lady. She was married and obviously not in Israel's leadership or in the thick of the battle in which they were engaged. In fact she was far from the scene of battle, going about her chores. She was, however, exactly where God wanted her to be in order for him to use her. Although at times life may seem humdrum – cleaning the house, for instance, or decorating a room or caring for a child – if you are where God wants you in obedience, he'll bless and use you right there.

Secondly, she was doubly blessed: she was blessed not only amongst women, but amongst tent-dwelling women. Not everyone lived in tents like Jael. There were cities and therefore houses, which would have been more comfortable and more protective. But tent-dwellers do not settle down. They are mobile and always ready to move, as was Abraham before her and the children of Israel themselves, who followed the pillar of cloud and fire at a moment's notice. Tent-dwellers may experience a certain amount of discomfort with the elements and the terrain, and may be more vulnerable, but they are alert and adaptable. Here, in Jael, the Lord is blessing an attitude. He commends her for relying on him for her protection and comfort, and not on the security of material things which can, in a moment, vanish and fail. He wants a people who are flexible enough to be able to move quickly at his bidding. The only reason that Jael was in that particular spot was because she and her husband Heber had left the rest of the Kenites, and were camping alone. There's nothing wrong with houses and possessions as such, but there may well be something wrong with our dependence upon them.

Thirdly, she killed the enemy with what she had. There was no time to wait for the warriors to return. There was no whining or hesitation because she didn't have a sword or spear or some other appropriate killing weapon. She saw God's enemy and used what was to hand – a tent peg and a mallet. She went quietly about her task – she made no song and dance to alert the enemy to her intention. She fearlessly drove that tent peg right through his head. The Lord is looking for people of faith and aggression, who will use whatever they have in their hands to make war on his enemies. These are not now flesh and blood like Sisera, but demons, principalities and powers who are nonetheless real.

Jael was indeed doubly blessed, but so can we be blessed if we take her example to heart. Be content with the situation God has placed you in; be ever ready to respond to the Spirit's prompting to action; and use whatever gifts and talents you have. Don't wait until you are better equipped or more informed or better trained before you enter the battle. Make yourself available now to hate and destroy God's enemies, and be blessed like Jael of old. May every one of us be soldiers for Christ.

Read: Judges 4:18-24; Joel 3:9-11; 2 Corinthians 10:1-6.

Consider and pray: Are you a little nervous when you consider entering the area of spiritual warfare? Do you feel inadequate and ill-equipped? There are three things I want you to pray about at this point. First, pray for a hatred and aggression towards Satan and the enemies of God's people. Second, pray for the grace to accept the place God has for you at this time, in spite of its limitations. Third, pray for strength to discover and use all the gifts and abilities the Lord has placed within you. If you are moving in obedience he will use and bless you right where you are.

20

The blessing of unity

For there the Lord bestows his blessing, even life for evermore.
Psalm 133:3

We have already seen that God our Father, through the sacrifice of Jesus his Son, has freely given to his children everlasting life. When we appreciate exactly what it was that happened at Calvary, we can begin to appropriate and draw upon God's many blessings in Christ. It's mind-boggling every time you think about this. Let me say it once more: Jesus became a curse for all mankind, so that the curse of sin could be lifted from us. Our response to this, having done nothing good in our lives, is to admit the truth of our failure and to accept Jesus' gift for ourselves – life for evermore. No wonder the Bible tells us that "the message of the cross is foolishness to those who are perishing, but to us who are being saved it is the power of God" (1 Corinthians 1:18). Surely, then, this life must be the greatest gift anyone can receive. Psalm 133 refers to this same gift, but sets it against a background of unity – a unity which, as scripture teaches us elsewhere, can only be achieved amongst those who have first been reconciled to God.

We in the church of Jesus Christ today see little enough of that commodity around. In fact, our disunity is a scandal and a talking-point for the world. In Britain at this present time we are hearing much through the media about Islam. Salman Rushdie's book, *The Satanic Verses*, has brought sharply into focus the intensity of feeling amongst Muslims about their religion. They are found universally decrying what they consider to be a blasphemous book and are one in their determination to see it banned. One of their statements which has hit me over and over again is the contrast which they draw between the Islamic togetherness and the Christian disunity and disorganisation. In some talk shows I have heard them laughing at the church's inability to show a united front, even about the foundation of its faith – the birth, life, death and resurrection of Jesus Christ.

What, then, is this elusive unity which is spoken of in our psalm? Well, it certainly cannot refer to doctrinal unity, because the Bible clearly teaches us that we grow into that kind of harmony; it comes with maturity. Furthermore, whilst I'm on the subject, some pretty diabolical things have been perpetrated in the name of doctrine. Over and over again throughout the history of the church, Christians have used violence towards one another, persecuting and martyring those who refused to conform. We are all familiar with the atrocities committed by the Inquisition, and even Martin Luther himself did some unspeakable things in the name of Jesus. Where were the "brothers living together in unity" in all that? I do understand that doctrine is vitally important, but our unity does not start there. Even the most ardent exponents of pet doctrines, when asked point-blank if they know they have finally arrived at total understanding, will *perhaps* reluctantly admit that they *possibly* have something to learn, although they can't imagine what! To say otherwise would be crassly proud. Why is it, then, that we don't act with more humility and admit that we do still have something to learn in this matter of dogma? Why do we get out our doctrinal daggers first and enquire last, often over a bleeding corpse, as to whether we are truly Christian brothers or not?

Jesus is coming back. He is returning to finally be wedded to his bride, the church. Christ the head will be seen to be one with his body. I believe that our psalm is looking forward to that great event and encouraging us to hasten the glorious day. Jesus is not coming back for a church full of schism, unable to distinguish brother from enemy. He is coming back for those who dwell together in unity, and amazingly enough, dwell means *dwell*! It does not mean meeting once or twice a week. When brothers dwell together, they live, speak, breathe, love and discipline together, sharing all their joys and sorrows. Dwelling together is a way of life, and only when we are living that kind of life will God bestow the fullness of his blessing.

Some versions of the Bible translate the phrase "bestows his blessing" as "commands his blessing". I like that. This kind of brotherly love provokes a response from God which cannot be rescinded. How should this affect ordinary saints like you and me? What can we do to help bring about this tangible evidence of our unity? Firstly, we can ask the Lord to share with us his overwhelming burden for oneness, as expressed in his prayer in John 17. Secondly, we can go out of our way to affirm whatever we see of Christ in our brothers and sisters. Thirdly, we can speak well of one another, at all times. Fourthly, we can

The blessing of unity

share our concerns in the scriptural manner, which Jesus gave us in Matthew 18:15-20. If we begin to live, using these simple guidelines, we will create an atmosphere where committed and loving relationships can flourish, where we can expect that God will *command* the blessing, even life for evermore.

Read: Psalm 133; John 17:20-26; Matthew 18:15-20.

Consider and pray: Think about the world-wide church, in all its diversity. Thank God for all his people, whatever their national or denominational background. Then ask the Lord to share with you his burden for unity in Spirit and in truth. Acknowledge that unity of Spirit is already ours in Jesus, and pray for strength to maintain this without compromise or favour. Seek his guidance as to how you can begin to get closer to those he has placed you with in your local church setting. Finally, endeavour to put things right where there has been broken fellowship, as far as you possibly can.

21
The beatitudes

"Blessed are the poor in spirit, for theirs is the kingdom of heaven. Blessed are those who mourn, for they will be comforted. Blessed are the meek, for they will inherit the earth. Blessed are those who hunger and thirst for righteousness, for they will be filled."

Matthew 5:3-6

When Jesus sat on the hillside and began to teach the large crowd which had followed him, I guess they understood him as little as we do today. They had just seen him perform miracles and were hoping to see more. They were hungry for the supernatural power of God in their lives. After all, the majority of them, as good Jews, had been brought up on the biblical stories which told how God's might had been exercised on behalf of his people. They regularly recalled, as part of their heritage, the accounts of the plagues in Egypt, the Red Sea crossing, the entry into the promised land and Jericho's fall. Now here was Jesus, another miracle worker. Undoubtedly God was with him.

They hung on to his every word but understood very little of what he said.

Who are these people Jesus spoke of, who are so blessed? Can we appropriate these blessings in our own lives? Everyone there would have understood the word "poor"; many of them would have been poor themselves. We in the affluent West may grasp the concept, but for very few of us is it a reality at any point in our lives, and seldom do our paths cross with the truly poor. But "poor in spirit" – what does that mean? Mourning, on the other hand, is something which touches most of our lives when we suffer bereavement and need comfort. But does the mere fact that we're mourning mean that we are candidates for God's blessing? In British society there are those who mourn inconsolably over cats, dogs and budgies. Are they included? "Meek" is a word that we don't often use. We are inclined to view meekness as synonymous with weakness. Surely weakness can never be a prerequisite for inheriting the earth? Again, being hungry and thirsty is outside of the experience of most of us. We're starving when lunch is held up for an hour. But "hunger and thirst for righteousness' sake" – that's another matter. Can we really hunger and thirst for that? Well, it does seem so, if we are to believe what the Bible tells us, and we are assured that that sort of emptiness is going to be filled.

It is my belief that in order to begin to understand the implications of these things, we must view and interpret them through the life of Jesus. He was not merely a teacher; he actually lived the life he spoke of, and that life is faithfully recorded in the Gospels. He is our pattern, our recipe. If you don't want your garment to be grotesque or your meal to be inedible, you follow the instructions. These instructions are discovered by watching closely our Lord's exemplary life and by studying the teaching he outlines in the whole of his sermon found in Matthew chapters 5-7.

Jesus was himself poor in spirit. When I look at his example, I find I'm rich in spirit. I make all kinds of judgments and decisions on my own account. But Jesus, who was full of the Holy Spirit, shows us the way. He said, "the Son can do nothing by himself; he can do only what he sees his Father doing" (John 5:19). We find it again in the prayer he taught his disciples to pray: "Your kingdom come, your will be done." The poor in spirit are those who know beyond question that their human resources can only fail and that it is God's Holy Spirit alone who can work through us to bring about the kingdom of heaven.

Jesus led the way too in hungering and thirsting for righteousness as he carried a burden for the poor. He fully understood God's heart for the needy and the under-privileged. He constantly made waves as he spoke out against injustice and inequality wherever he saw it. We must do the same. Giving lip-service to the idea of the equality of all men is not enough. We must have fire in our hearts which compels us into action.

Jesus did not die and rise again merely for white, middle-class, thrifty and whole people. He also died and rose for people of all colours, for the unemployed, for the handicapped; each one has the same value before the throne of his grace. It is a measure of the righteousness in our society that the most dangerous place for a child to be is in its mother's womb, particularly if that child has any diagnosable deformity or deficiency. Wherever we see discrimination of any kind – in schools, buses, shops, government, newspapers, public offices – let us be ravenous to see righteousness prevail in our land, for all people, whoever they may be.

So these blessings cannot come as a result of holding earthly values, for heaven is their source. To be truly poor in spirit is to totally trust our heavenly Father as Jesus did; to mourn is to weep for the things that Jesus wept for; to be meek is to be broken in, obediently receiving his yoke; and to hunger and thirst for righteousness is to long for God's justice to fill the earth and to work towards that goal.

We must never allow the blessing of God to become remote from us. Rather, let us cooperate with the Holy Spirit to gain a greater understanding of how Jesus sees the world in which we live, and of how he views the many peoples who inhabit our planet. So, following in his steps, let us be doers of his word and not simply readers or hearers. In order to be effective, his word needs a body. That's why Jesus came as man, and that's why he looks for men and women today. Now he is no longer here in person; we are his representatives and the members of his body. We, corporately, are Christ incarnate; he lives through us, ruling and reigning to establish his kingdom amongst us.

Read: John 5:16-30; James 2:1-9; Psalm 72:1-4.

Consider and pray: Come before the Lord in meekness and humility, asking him to remove the mystery which veils his words. Ask him to help you understand for yourself what it means to be poor in spirit, to mourn, to be meek and to hunger and thirst for righteousness. He will not crush you with this revelation, for the Spirit is not only our teacher but also our comforter. Remember that his objective is blessing – he wants to bless you and those whom you move amongst in your family, your church and the world at large.

22
Multiplied blessings!

"Blessed are the merciful, for they will be shown mercy. Blessed are the pure in heart, for they will see God. Blessed are the peacemakers, for they will be called sons of God. Blessed are those who are persecuted because of righteousness, for theirs is the kingdom of heaven. Blessed are you when people insult you, persecute you and falsely say all kinds of evil against you because of me. Rejoice and be glad, because great is your reward in heaven, for in the same way they persecuted the prophets who were before you."

Matthew 5:7-12

Let us continue to think about these teachings of Jesus. I'm afraid I'm not qualified, nor is there space here, to give you an exhaustive, word-by-word, Bible study. I simply want to share some of my own thoughts with you. I trust that they will challenge and stimulate you to find out more and to grasp for yourself these wonderful blessings of God. You are allowed to be greedy for more of him, and jealous for more and more of his blessings.

Multiplied blessings!

When we read this passage of scripture, I'm sure that we all thrill to the words and their promise of blessing, and we hopefully aspire to the heavenly attributes. For many of us, however, the reality falls far short even of our aims and objectives. One of the causes for this failure is that in our minds we place these things beyond our reach. We view them as holy ideals, which are almost irrelevant to us and our daily living. So we don't actually apply them to ourselves.

I once had to undergo surgery at very short notice and found myself in hospital. On that Monday morning I had gone to my doctor; my appointment was for 10:00 a.m. My condition was serious, and by lunchtime I had been admitted. During the three weeks I was there, many women came in, had their abortions and went home, mostly on the same day. One girl had left it rather late in her pregnancy. She had to be induced and actually go through the labour. All on the ward, staff and patients included, were disturbed by this particular case. In order to show their disapproval, the staff did only what was necessary, and then left this young woman in a side room to face things alone. The girl had no idea what she was going to have to go through as a result of her decision to get rid of the baby.

Everyone by now knew what I felt about the subject, and also about my faith. I radically disagreed with the regular Tuesday and Thursday slaying of infants. Nevertheless, I went in and sat with the girl, talking to her, rubbing her back and just being there. Disagreeing with someone's actions does not automatically mean you should divorce yourself from that person and their pain. The opportunity to show mercy, rather than righteous indignation, was well within my grasp in that situation. From that simple kindness I had many opportunities to speak to the woman about Jesus. As Christians we should understand the power of the godly attribute of mercy. Jesus died for me while I was a sinner! How glad we are to apply his mercy to ourselves. We should not be slow about showing it to others.

Jesus spent time and ate meals with outcasts. He did not believe that by associating with them he would share the guilt of their sins. He had come to bring peace between God and man. He was not a peacekeeper as we are at times, when we duck the issues in our families, marriages and churches and do anything for a quiet life – he was a peacemaker! That cost him blood! We usually don't want to rock the boat. Rather than face up to a situation (perhaps for the tenth time), we stay silent in order to keep the peace.

I find that many Christians need help to be at peace with God. During a young people's meeting at which John and I had been asked to speak, there were a number of words of knowledge, some on the subject of abortion. Many girls came forward to be prayed for as a result of these words. Whilst all this was going on the Lord put something in my heart which was directed to the young men in the congregation. I simply said that God held them accountable for their careless attitude towards their own seed. For most of us abortion has a female face and we tend to forget that a male is always involved. I prayed with one particular fellow. God had shown him that his restlessness and backsliding were direct results of his thoughtlessness and irresponsibility. Amidst tears of repentance, peace was restored between this young man and God. I did not find it easy to say what I said, but it was the key to peace for some of those young men.

The beatitudes are not just wonderful words, they are chock-a-block with challenges for us which lead to blessing. In the last meditation I wrote about righteousness and our actions towards the poor. Here the subject of righteousness pops up again. Now, however, we are to contemplate persecution as a result of righteousness. Today some people are in prison for protesting against unjust laws which penalise the poor. In some countries, others have even died for their stand against racial prejudice. Many of those who suffer in this way are not Christians, but they are men and women of good will. They care about injustice, poverty, oppression and empty stomachs. They put us to shame, as we in the church of Jesus Christ should be the trend-setters, not the tail-end Charlies.

Persecution is not something which I relish. In fact I feel sure I'd be one of the first to run for cover if it started happening here. God understands this. All he requires of us is our trust and willingness to cooperate with him. We are to walk in truth, one day at a time, and he will supply the grace to see us through, whatever may come our way.

What can I say about these last blessings? Perhaps we have examples in our own lives of receiving spite and animosity, more often because of our own folly than for the Lord's sake. Let's face it, we Christians can be an extremely miserable and negative bunch. Our faith has, at times, been reduced to a long list of "do nots", and we have been guilty of taking all the fun and enjoyment out of life. Being accused of eccentricity or prudery or being a kill-joy is not exactly what Jesus is speaking of here.

There is a dimension of suffering for the sake of the gospel which we in this country have not encountered. We surely must not go looking for it, but it is a promise of God if we are beatitude people. In all of these things we are finally called to rejoice and be glad. Not because we will own a wonderful home, or have a totally Christian family, or be able to give away lots of money to the poor, or any of a hundred and one other good things. But we are to rejoice and be glad because we will find ourselves in excellent company – that of our brethren, the prophets, who suffered in the same way.

Now have come the salvation and the power and the kingdom of our God, and the authority of his Christ. For the accuser of our brothers, who accuses them before our God day and night, has been hurled down. They overcame him by the blood of the Lamb and by the word of their testimony; they did not love their lives so much as to shrink from death.

Revelation 12:10-11

Read: 2 Timothy 3:10-13; Romans 2:1-16.

Consider and pray: There are many areas in these beatitudes to challenge us, perhaps even to bring us to our knees before the Lord. The whole subject of judgment and mercy, and the way in which we have applied these in the past, may need repentance on our part. Maybe you have been a peace*keeper* and need to find God's strength to change. It will cost you pain and the risk of rejection to be a peace*maker* like Jesus. Whatever God is saying to you in your heart, turn now to prayer. Reject condemnation and receive the Lord's encouragement to go forward in his strength. Pray for those who are experiencing suffering at this present moment, that God will sustain them.

23

The lesson of Mary

*"From now on all generations will call me blessed, for the
Mighty One has done great things for me – holy is his name."*
Luke 1:48-49

Surely this must be one of the most outstanding examples
of receiving the will of God as a blessing. Mary not only
accepted it for the duration of her natural life, but also
throughout the ages to come. Blessing is released in our
lives by hearing and obeying the voice of God. This shows
that we believe that God really does know what he's doing,
even when we cannot understand exactly how he is going
to bring his word to pass.

Take a look at Mary's background and the reception she
gave to God's news. She was the product of a culture,
religion and tradition that valued women almost solely for
their virginity and their childbearing ability. When the
angel Gabriel came, her response was overwhelming. He
announced that she would bear a child. She did not reply
as many of us would, "Oh, please, not that! What will
people think?" But, rather, she responded with a quiet,

"How will this be, since I am a virgin?" Amazingly, Gabriel's reply answered all her doubts: "The Holy Spirit will come upon you, and you will conceive." Of course, we know how the whole chain of events worked out, but Mary had no idea how the story would end. She simply said "Yes" to God and accepted his word as blessing.

Mary's news must have come as a shock to her family. Imagine the utter disbelief there would be if someone in your home were to make such an announcement. She was engaged and had not had intercourse with Joseph; he would be positive that the baby was not his. There was no assurance at the time that he would understand. Mary alone had heard the voice of God. Sure enough, Joseph's first reaction was to very quietly put her away. He obviously cared deeply, as he did not want to make a public spectacle of her. It was only later that he had his own revelation through a dream. Then he finally understood and went through with the marriage.

This baby was not born a decent nine months after the wedding; he was already on the way at the time of that event. You can read between the lines in the Gospels the little hints which were made about Jesus' untimely arrival. A son was usually identified by placing the father's name alongside the child's – hence, Jesus the Son of Joseph. However, at times we read of him being called Mary's son. This, in effect, was a "nudge, nudge, wink, wink", and a sly reference to the manner of his birth. No doubt someone would say, "Wasn't there trouble in the family?" or "Didn't he come rather fast on the heels of the wedding?" His parentage was called into question when they referred to him as Mary's son, and this must have caused her great pain, casting a slur on her character.

Mary's faith in God's word kept her through all the joys and difficulties surrounding Jesus' birth and childhood:

the visits of the shepherds and the wise men; the flight into Egypt; the stories which must have filtered through about the terrible slaughter of the innocent babies. She was steadfast and continued in the blessing of God, faithful to what she had heard at each stage of Jesus' eventful life. She saw him through his circumcision and the incident in the temple; she was present at his first miracle at the wedding in Cana, and she looked on when he preached in his home town. She was there at the cross and at the tomb and again in the upper room. Nothing the enemy threw across her path could deter her, and we never hear of her being bitter or blaming God or giving up. Through pain, suffering, misunderstanding, death and resurrection Mary counted herself blessed. She was always there.

Her secret, then, was in hearing God and steadfastly believing that, come what may, he only does wonderful things. What an example Mary is for us to follow. How we fail in appreciating her and proclaiming her to be blessed of God. Truly blessed is Mary the mother of our Lord Jesus Christ, who heard from God and never wavered. We now have the assurance of Jesus himself that he will never leave us, but nowhere does he promise us a smooth ride. He never said that we won't be unjustly accused or that our friends won't desert us. He gave no guarantee that everything we do will always be successful. He does not offer us eternal youth and perfect bodies in this life. What he does promise is that when God speaks to us, we, as his sheep, will hear his voice. He has also given us the Holy Spirit to enable us to be faithful witnesses like Mary. His words are to be relied upon and his blessings are true. May we be found in the company of Mary and many of the saints, as part of that throng who count themselves blessed of God to have encountered some hardships for the sake of Jesus and his gospel.

Past Perfect

Let me close with the story of one such modern-day saint. Whilst in India in 1989 John and I spent some time visiting some of the village churches which were under the leadership of an Indian friend. The majority of these people could neither read nor write, nor did they have a Bible of their own. Yet their faith was remarkable, even in the face of outright persecution. One woman who asked me to pray for her had a testimony which challenged me to the core. Her large family of children, who had all accepted Jesus with her, were in a boat on the river. A Hindu priest who was the worse for drink threatened to turn the boat over unless they denied Christ. They refused to do this, so he capsized the boat. All the children were drowned, together with the priest himself. The villagers carried the bodies to the woman's hut and mocked her. "See how strong the Hindu gods are!" they cried. "No," she replied through her tears, "see how powerful Jesus is. He has taken my children to a place where they can never be hurt again."

Read: Luke 1:26-38 & 46-56; Psalm 86:1-13.

Consider and pray: God's ways are not always clear to us, and blessings once given can easily fade into mists of confusion if we let them go. One thing is sure, however: God wants to bless us and will use anything and everything he can to achieve that end. Consciously acknowledge God's promises to you in the past – even write them down. List his blessings and at the same time open your mind and heart for him to speak fresh words of reassurance to you right now. Stand on the things he has said and build on them, so that you are not found to be living on the shifting sands of mere experience, but on the living, lasting word of God.

100

24

God's bias to the poor

A generous man will himself be blessed, for he shares his food with the poor.

Proverbs 22:9

"Is not this the kind of fasting I have chosen . . . to share your food with the hungry and to provide the poor wanderer with shelter – when you see the naked, to clothe him, and not to turn away from your own flesh and blood?"

Isaiah 58:6-7

God has a special place in his heart for the poor. The Scriptures challenge us to scrutinise our attitude towards them. What's more, there is a strong link between the outpouring of God's blessing and the way we treat the poor. It seems clear to me that the Lord has a bias towards the poor. In fact I'm sure that this is the case, for the poor have no-one to plead for them and their lives are constantly in danger. Of course, God is not more concerned for the poor than he is for the rich when it comes to his saving grace. All are welcome, for when any man sees his own spiritual poverty and need of a saviour, God is ready to receive him. In Revelation 3 the Lord declares the rich Laodicean church to be "wretched, pitiful, poor, blind and naked". However, in both the Old and New Testaments the needs of the visibly poor – the orphaned, the widows, the underprivileged and the disadvantaged – are clearly identified for us and demand a response.

The new church of Jesus was birthed with a commission to minister to the poor, and it immediately began to make provision for them. In the early chapters of the Acts of the Apostles we read that it was considered of prime importance for the twelve to give themselves to the ministry of the word. Consequently such duties as waiting on tables and distributing to the poor widows had to be delegated. The highest qualifications were required for this work. Those chosen would have to be full of the Holy Spirit, wisdom and faith. The Lord obviously rated serving the poor extremely highly.

When I visited India I fell in love with the people and the place. The poverty there was totally overwhelming. I soon discovered that one would require the wisdom of Solomon to sort out those who were poor from those who made a good living by begging; there was a vast difference. One would also need faith to meet the very real needs of these people. Without the Holy Spirit, you would not know where to begin. However, we don't have to board an aeroplane to find the poor. They are all around us – even on our own doorstep.

I have found Isaiah 58 particularly provocative, especially verse 7. This verse took on a totally new meaning for me when I realised that the flesh and blood that Isaiah was referring to was not only that of my own family. Here the prophet was speaking of all humanity. Jesus himself pointed our way when he asked the question, "Who is my mother and who are my brothers?" He certainly wasn't rejecting his natural mother and brothers, but he was enlarging our horizons. He was sharpening our sense of responsibility to include all men and women with whom we share our basic humanity.

There is so much deprivation in the world that we will need God's help and guidance to begin to work against it. We are often told that not everyone is required to sell everything they possess and give it all away, and I suppose that it wouldn't make sense if we did. Perhaps we would simply be adding our own families to the ranks of the poor. Nevertheless, I do believe we should be much more willing to think about selling any surplus we may have and using it to bless the poor. Sadly, many people are threatened by such thoughts, and we need to understand that God is not looking for reluctant, unconvinced givers. He is not seeking to prise our possessions away from us. I'm not even saying that saving is a bad thing. In fact, these days it can be extremely helpful if it keeps you out of debt. Saving rather than buying first and paying later can be good stewardship. But I'm sure God may want to say something to us about accumulating money for the sake of safety, or for a rainy day. We are plainly told not to worry about tomorrow, and doesn't that include the massive preparations of many people for retirement? God will undoubtedly continue to make provision for us as long as we are hearing him about our finances and possessions.

To ignore or to become hardened to the fate of our fellow human beings brings God's judgment upon us. Matthew 25 underlines the fact that feeding the hungry, giving drink to the thirsty, welcoming the stranger, tending the sick and visiting those in prison should be a part of everyday living in our churches and fellowships. So much so, that when the Lord commends it as being something special, those involved are surprised: "When did we do those things?" Jesus said that the poor would always be with us. This should draw from us concern and compassion rather than impatience and a desire to ignore their existence. As we read on in our Isaiah 58 passage, we see that God's blessings are boundless when we find our way into his heart in this matter: "Then your light will break forth like the dawn, and your healing will quickly appear; then your righteousness will go before you, and the glory of the Lord will be your rearguard" (verse 8).

Read: Isaiah 58:6-12; 2 Corinthians 9:6-15; Luke 16:19-31.

Consider and pray: As you come to prayer about the issues of poverty and wealth and your response to the poor, you must lay aside all fears and misunderstandings about God's motives for you. Past pressures and a warped understanding of his heart will lead you to close up or move out of a false sense of duty. Blessing is his goal; he wants to bless both the poor and you. He is not out to rob you but to draw you into an understanding of the truth that it is more blessed to give than to receive. Those who find the secret of joy-filled giving are blessed indeed. Of course, money is not all that we can give: time, prayers and spiritual gifts are also amongst the many things the Lord entrusts to us to pass on to others.

25

The blessing of multiplication

God blessed them and said to them, "Be fruitful and increase in number; fill the earth and subdue it."

Genesis 1:28

The very first thing God did after he had created Adam and Eve was to bless them. His work was absolutely perfect and good, and he wanted more of the same. So he blessed them and told them to multiply. Later, at the time of Noah, he looked with such great sadness upon the terrible harvest which was the outcome of our first parents' sin. So great was the disobedience and the rejection of his word through Noah, that he had no alternative but to blot mankind out and start all over again with Noah and his family. Consistently throughout Scripture we see God taking the few in order to increase them and bless the many. There was Abraham, there was Gideon with his tiny band, and there was Jesus with a mere handful of disciples. In Genesis 9 there is a new beginning, and God blesses Noah and his sons and tells them to multiply. So one of God's rich blessings is the power to multiply.

We can also see this in the family scene. The Bible tells us that "children are a reward from the Lord" and that "blessed is the man whose quiver is full of them" (Psalm 127). When you consider how vastly underpopulated the world was, with at first only two people, Adam and Eve, and later just eight including Noah, you can see that children were indeed a blessing. The more the merrier. But things have changed since then with the tremendous population explosion. If we all took this multiplication commandment literally, there would soon be standing room only. Of course, children are still a great blessing. But there is also spiritual significance to the command to multiply, which is reflected in Jesus, commission to "go and make disciples of all nations" (Matthew 28:19).

In the Old Testament, God chose a nation through which to display his blessings. That nation, Israel, was to be an example and a source of wonder to the whole earth. They were to multiply and be a channel for the glory of God. Tragically, they failed to recognise their Messiah when he came. They had a form of godliness but denied the power, and so God had to reject them as the example, and he started small once again. Already his plans were under way when he called a young virgin girl, Mary. Her son was God's only Son, who submitted himself to his Father. He called twelve men to be with him, and so the circle was beginning to grow once more.

As we continue through the Gospels and on into the Acts of the Apostles, we see more of this divine multiplication. Soon there are seventy. Jesus dies and his followers are smitten and shattered. But by the time we come to the upper room there are one hundred and twenty. Then the Holy Spirit comes, catapulting them out into the streets. Suddenly the growth moves into a new dimension, as the multiplication leaps to almost thirty times. It is clear that

God is no longer looking for birth solely in the natural realm. In Christ there is a second birth as men become totally new creatures born of the Spirit. Now we are not just one physical nation, but a spiritual people drawn from every tribe and tongue – a generation reproducing after their own kind, filled with the Holy Spirit and longing to pass on this pulsating life to those who are dead in their trespasses and sin.

Jesus' command to "go into all the world and preach the gospel" must be viewed alongside the Genesis command to be fruitful and multiply. If a lack of children under the old covenant was a sign of God withholding his blessing, so barrenness in our church life today must have much more to say to us. This is not said to condemn, but rather to encourage us to seek God for the reason. Any couple who are unable to have natural children seek the doctor's help to find out why. There may be some simple explanation, and treatment brings about the desired pregnancy. Should we do less than to seek the Lord as to why our lives and churches are fruitless and barren? Certainly, we know that the Great Physician, Jesus, longs for us to bear fruit and that our fruit should remain (John 15:16).

I was speaking with one of the leaders of a new church, quite close to where we live. In twelve months, since the new leadership team came into being, the numbers of committed people have doubled and they are expecting them to double again within the next year also. They believe that God will bless them in this way, and I pray that their faith will be rewarded. In this country, where for so many Christians "small is beautiful", we especially need to know that one of God's blessings is multiplication. Whether the ones and twos of friendship evangelism, or the larger numbers as the result of a concerted effort or campaign, or the massive growth of revival – all are signs of healthy, thriving churches.

Read: John 1:10-13 & 15:1-17.

Consider and pray: God has a heart for the world, and so he sent Jesus for all men everywhere. Growth is the natural outcome of a right relationship to him. Are there blockages in our spiritual reproductive system? Many things can contribute to barrenness: fear of failure, self-centredness, hypocrisy, introversion, unbelief, deception, a wrong gospel – the list is endless. But our God has a history of changing the fortunes of those who humbly seek his face. There is no condition which he cannot deal with except determined apathy and lukewarmness. Let the Holy Spirit minister faith to you, and resolve to sow your seed liberally.

> "Sing, O barren woman, you who never bore a child; burst into song, shout for joy, you who were never in labour, because more are the children of the desolate woman than of her who has a husband," says the Lord.
> Isaiah 54:1

26
Spiritual blessings

Praise be to the God and Father of our Lord Jesus Christ, who has blessed us in the heavenly realms with every spiritual blessing in Christ . . . Having believed, you were marked in him with a seal, the promised Holy Spirit, who is a deposit guaranteeing our inheritance until the redemption of those who are God's possession – to the praise of his glory.

Ephesians 1:3, 13-14

When Jesus was on the earth, he made a commitment to his disciples that he would never leave them. However, he knew that in the confines of his earthly body he would be too restricted, as he could only be in one place at a time. After his resurrection he appeared bodily to his followers first here and then there, never simultaneously in several places at once. In John 16 he prepared his disciples for his departure by explaining that the Holy Spirit would come in his place. His provision was that the Comforter would be with all his people, all of the time, wherever they were. There was no need to get in line or wait your turn, nor did they have to be in deep trouble to gain his attention. Through Christ the blessings which the Holy Spirit brings are released to all Christians everywhere, without limitation.

This is a totally new state of affairs. In the Old Testament, the Spirit of God came upon specific people at different times. If we look at the life of Saul, for instance, we can see that after Samuel anointed him with oil (1 Samuel 10), the Spirit came upon him, and he joined with a band of prophets to prophesy with them. Later he lost God's blessing because of his sin. The Spirit of God left him (1 Samuel 16) and tragically, in his place, the Lord sent an evil spirit to torment Saul, in the hope that this might cause him to turn back to God again and receive forgiveness. Similarly, the Holy Spirit frequently came on Samson, enabling him to perform his mighty deeds. Elisha even claimed a double portion of the Spirit from Elijah his master. But at best, in those times, God's evident presence was spasmodic and limited.

Nevertheless, there were promises in the Old Testament of a change to come. In Isaiah 44:3 we read, "I will pour out my Spirit on your offspring, and my blessing on your descendants." Also in Joel 2:28-29: "I will pour out my Spirit on all people. Your sons and daughters will prophesy, your old men will dream dreams, your young men will see visions. Even on my servants, both men and women, I will pour out my Spirit in those days." These were wonderful promises of God's blessing to come. Jesus was the first man to be full of the Holy Spirit, receiving the blessing without measure and in a unique way. At his baptism the heavens opened, the dove descended and the voice of his Father spoke: "This is my Son, whom I love; with him I am well pleased" (Matthew 3:17).

Jesus was the new Adam, all things related to the old Adam being fulfilled and ended in him. In addition, he was the first of a new humanity, a generation of men and women who, like Jesus, were filled with the Holy Spirit. They would follow in his steps, whatever the personal cost. The price for Jesus was high. He would die a criminal's death in order to release for all mankind, from that moment on until the end of time, the exchange of everlasting life for death. He needed the Holy Spirit to complete the job his Father had entrusted to him, and we too need that same Holy Spirit today to fulfil the tasks that God has prepared in advance for us to do (Ephesians 2:10).

It was necessary for the Lord to return to his Father, so that the Holy Spirit could come. At his ascension (Acts 1:7-10), he told the disciples to go back to Jerusalem and wait there for the promised Holy Spirit. They obeyed him, and when they were all met together in one place the Spirit came with wind and fire, turning their lives upside down. They were never the same again. This truly was the birth of the triumphant church of Jesus Christ. He had promised that he would build her and that not even the gates of hell would be able to stand against her.

Do you see that now, because we are in Christ and are partakers of the same Spirit that raised him from the dead, we are seated with him in heavenly places? Because we yield our lives to him, he is able to live through us, giving us a share in his throne of authority. Yes, there is no question that God has blessed us with every spiritual blessing in the heavenly realms. What a privilege to be a co-worker with the Lord Jesus and the Holy Spirit in God's building project!

Read: Ephesians 1:3-14; Acts 2:38-39; Revelation 12:7-11.

Consider and pray: The spiritual realm which is opened up to us by the Holy Spirit may be a subject which brings fear or confusion to you. But God only wants to do you good. The characteristics of the Spirit are seen in wind, fire, water, oil and dove. Whilst the Holy Spirit is unpredictable, he brings only blessing to those who want God. His presence is purging, refreshing and healing and brings peace beyond our comprehension. We cannot survive without him, and he lifts us into the heavenly places from whence we can live above the dictates of worldly appetites and temptations. Open yourself up to the Holy Spirit and pray for him to come to you in a new way to empower you for victory and service.

27
Supernatural gifts

Now to each one the manifestation of the Spirit is given for the common good.

1 Corinthians 12:7

Let's think a little more about spiritual blessings. It is clear from the passage in Ephesians (1:3, 13-14) that there is an obvious relationship between "blessings in the heavenly realms" and having "the seal of the promised Holy Spirit". He is sent to us from the throne, lifts us to the throne and manifests the power of the throne through us here on earth. It is impossible to separate the Holy Spirit from his gifts; they are part and parcel of the spiritual blessings which the Lord bestows upon his people. They are not an end in themselves but a means to an end – that is, "the common good".

Many questions are asked about the way the Holy Spirit works through us today. Some say his gifts are not applicable at this time; some say that they very definitely are. It seems to me that if God the Father knew that his only Son Jesus could not begin his ministry without the Holy Spirit and his gifts, and that if Jesus knew that his church could not commence without the Spirit and the gifts, then surely we can't continue the work which they started unless we have that same power. Personally, I am convinced that I need all the help I can get in my battle with the enemy.

Jesus is building his church, but it isn't a bricks and mortar job. It involves real, live people being built together in such a way that nothing the enemy can throw at them will succeed in bringing them down. The Lord promised that he would send the Holy Spirit to help us, so I fully expect him to do just that. The Holy Spirit comes firstly to give us the power to live holy lives by dealing with sin and temptations. Secondly, he comes to enable us to be witnesses in word, works and wonders (Romans 15:18-19), distributing his gifts so that the power of God's coming kingdom may be seen in the church by the world.

The reason I say this is because that is exactly the pattern we see in Jesus. Initially the Spirit came upon him, driving him into the wilderness, where he overcame the temptations of Satan. Only then did he begin his ministry, with all those miraculous signs following his preaching and teaching of God's word. In John 14:12 Jesus said, "I tell you the truth, anyone who has faith in me will do what I have been doing. He will do even greater things than these, because I am going to the Father." Later, in verse 16, he continued, "and I will ask the Father, and he will give you another Counsellor to be with you forever – the Spirit of truth". Jesus' promises are true and can be trusted; they have never been rescinded.

Spiritual gifts are supernatural weapons and are vitally necessary, because we do not fight flesh and blood, but principalities and powers (Ephesians 6:12). Let me give you just one illustration from the many I have experienced. I had a phone call from a friend whom I had prayed with some time before. She had been terrified of flying and was unable to do anything whilst in the air except cling to her husband, burying her nails in his arms. So they never went on long journeys. I felt that the Holy Spirit enabled me to discern a curse at work in her. Obviously, unless you are a "jet-setter", you don't tend to fly that often, so she had to wait for the opportunity to test the effectiveness of my prayers. She called to tell me that they had worked remarkably! On the way to the USA with her family, as she boarded the aircraft she felt the Lord speak to her. He said he was going to make it very clear to her that she was completely delivered – he certainly did. On the way out they flew into some turbulence and, as she put it, she felt not a flicker of fear. On the return journey the Lord spoke again, saying that he was going to underline to her that the curse was no more. This time they flew into a storm. Everything had to be tied down – even the cabin attendants were strapped firmly into their seats. But still my friend felt no fear. Her husband could not believe the change in his wife. The Holy Spirit had moved through me with his gifts for the common good.

Through the variety of gifts which the Holy Spirit distributes to God's people, many of the curses which plague us – fears, sicknesses, superstitions, demons and habits, to name but a few – are removed. We are blessed, God is glorified and the world sees that Jesus is alive. Obviously, I have not covered the work of the Holy Spirit in detail here. If you would like to read more on this subject, John and I have written a book entitled *Everyman's Guide to the Holy Spirit – the End of the World and You*, published by Kingsway. I'm sure you'll find it a helpful volume.

Read: 1 Corinthians 12:1-11; John 14:9-18.

Consider and pray: I mentioned Romans 15:18-19, where Paul describes how he "fully proclaimed the gospel of Christ". It was through the *words* he spoke, the *works* he accomplished and the *wonders* of miracles wrought by his hands, all in the power of the Holy Spirit. In order for us to fully proclaim the gospel, we too need this three-fold testimony of speech, deeds and signs inspired by the Holy Spirit. Pray for yourself, your local church and the church at large that we might see a greater measure of this anointing released in us all. Do not limit the Lord as to how he can use you. Desire the spiritual gifts and pray for the motivation of Christ's love and compassion.

28
The priestly blessing

"The Lord bless you and keep you; the Lord make his face shine upon you and be gracious to you; the Lord turn his face towards you and give you peace."

Numbers 6:24-26

These are very well-known verses from the Bible. Many non-Christians would recognise them, having heard them during their brief visits to church for christenings, weddings and funerals. I do believe that the Lord wanted these words to be of great significance, because of the blessing they invoked upon Israel. How tragic it is that nowadays they are so often misused, merely spoken as a signing-off point at the end of a service or church event. They were to be reserved solely to bless Israel, God's nation, which was holy to him. Now they are devalued, being used in inappropriate situations, even spoken over non-believers. This must grieve the Lord. We need to restore their meaning and power.

It might be interesting to ask a group of people – in Romford market-place for example, where I live – what

they understand about blessing and cursing. I believe they
would be quite familiar with the concept of curses and
incantations – in fact, with the satanic side of the supernatural. Films and TV have a high content of witches,
ghosts, ghouls, vampires, wizards, horror, ritual murder
and the whole range of paranormal phenomena. People
imbibe these ideas from both large and small screens,
opening themselves up to these foul practices, which
ultimately have an effect on their lives. Occasionally good
or white magic is presented, but it is the thin end of a very
thick wedge. Occultists consider it a weak expression of
their craft and serious disciples need to progress to the
more powerful practices. Amazingly, very few people
would have any knowledge of blessing. At best they would
translate this as being showered with things in a mater-
ialistic sense. I wonder how much these worldly concepts
have been infiltrated into the church – perhaps sub-
consciously, but even deliberately by some?

What then, are we invoking through this Aaronic blessing? I believe that overall, it is inviting God's holy presence into the lives of men and women. "The Lord bless
and keep you" – these words conjure up a picture in my
mind. I see God as our Father, treating us as favourite
daughters or sons. When anything comes near that looks
like harming us, he treads on it, killing it and discarding it.
We never know about these hundreds of incidents during
our lifetimes when we are preserved from danger. Occasionally we may have what we would term a "near miss" –
perhaps when we're crossing the road, in the car or
swimming in the sea we are suddenly aware of God's
intervention. Our heart beats faster and we're conscious
that a disaster has been averted. How the Lord blesses us
and keeps us constantly from both physical and spiritual
harm! And even when Satan does breach our defenses, our

Father is there, turning our pain and trials to good effect. We need to be much more thankful for his presence and interest in our daily lives.

"The Lord make his face shine upon you and be gracious to you" – again, in my picture, our Father begins to take on a tangible form. He's a silhouette against a shining, blinding light which is radiating from his face, but his back is turned towards us. This reminds me of Moses in Exodus 33:19-23, when he asks to see the glory of the Lord. He was placed in a cleft in the rock, and God covered him with his hand, only removing it once he had passed by. So Moses saw only the back view of God, since at that time a clear sight of God's face would have been too much even for Moses. Now God is being gracious to us. He is listening to our requests and replying to our petitions. This is a stage where a greater sense of God's immanence develops in our lives. There's a progression from the first picture of an unseen God, to a second of his radiant back view.

"The Lord turn his face towards you and give you peace" – this is the final and almost overwhelming phase. Our Father has turned towards us, with all his glory, bathing us in liquid golden fire. At this point I am conscious that we could be either utterly consumed, leaving not an atom behind, or we could revel in the unutterable peace that comes with seeing God face to face. It is his grace that enables us to survive. It is not only the Lord who has changed his position in each picture; we too have changed ours. We began, as it were, sitting in a room, enjoying the perfume of someone who was approaching. Next, we were on our knees with arms outstretched in supplication, waiting to receive from the hands of our God, who had not yet turned towards us. Finally we stand looking into his face, seeing his love and his longing for

119

fellowship, experiencing his care for his creation and his fatherhood. All this is revealed in his lovely face.

This Old Testament blessing is now made available to the church through Jesus Christ. It is for all those who are seeking to follow in his footsteps. There is so much for us to reclaim from Satan. He has robbed us of a large portion of our inheritance. As we identify these things, so we battle in order to regain them. Obeying God's word, trusting the Holy Spirit to instruct and guide us, keeping short accounts through repentance and forgiveness – these are all part of a process which ensures us a closer walk with the Lord. Listening to him takes time and practice, as it does not come naturally to us at first. So much of our communication is mixed in with our own thoughts and desires, hang-ups and misconceptions, but God is good. Because of our insecurity he takes time with each of us. He is the perfect Father and is totally committed to us.

Read: Exodus 33:12-21; Matthew 7:7-12; Psalm 86:5-13.

Consider and pray: Meditate on the priestly blessing. See that it was God's own words given to bless his people. If you love and trust in Jesus, these words are for you. Receive them, bask in God's presence and feel his peace flooding over you as you gaze into his face. He's the Lord God Almighty, but he's your loving Father too. He'll keep you, he'll shine on you, he'll be gracious to you and he'll give you peace. Amen!

29

Before the end comes

When Haman entered, the king asked him, "What should be done for the man the king delights to honour."

Esther 6:6

The Book of Esther, apart from the historical events it records, is full of types and shadows. All of them have their limitations and must be viewed in the light of the scripture, but they can help us in our understanding of this story. One such is Haman, the archetype of our enemy, Satan. Another is Mordecai who, in many ways, pictures the work of the Holy Spirit. He steers Esther along the right pathway, in relation both to the king and to the world outside the palace. That exactly reflects the Holy Spirit's job. He keeps us in close contact with the Lord and keeps our hearts soft towards the lost of the world, who are heading towards death and destruction. I find the Book of Esther both challenging and inspiring. One day I would love to write a play about the whole story, but for now there is just one aspect that I want to look at, and you'll find it recounted in chapter 6.

Past Perfect

So many blessings are promised in the Bible, particularly for those who stand against the devil and his temptations. He, like wicked Haman, often appears to be in total control. However real this may at times seem, it is completely untrue. Just when he really believes that he has us in a corner, God steps in and simply removes the prize from his grasping hands. Even his ultimate weapon, death, is but a shadow for those who trust the Lord. At this point in the narrative the king is unable to sleep and calls for the records to be read to him. As he listens, he discovers that he has never rewarded Mordecai for his action in averting an assassination attempt on himself.

The king calls Haman and asks him how such a man should be rewarded. Haman, in his arrogance, mistakenly thinks that the king is alluding to him, and gives his advice accordingly. He suggests that this person should be dressed in one of the king's own robes, sat upon the king's own horse and led through the streets by a prince. As they progress through the city, the prince should proclaim, for all to hear, why this man is being honoured. How like Satan this is! He is constantly attempting to dress up as king, desperate to receive honour and adulation. It was a great shock to Haman when he was given the task of so honouring Mordecai. After all, he had recently built a gallows in his garden, and was at that very moment on his way to ask the king for permission to hang Mordecai on it when this awful thing happened to him. The exciting promise that I see here is that God is going to make a public show of his love and blessing towards us, whilst the enemy has to walk at our side, powerless and seething with rage.

At the end of chapter 6, Haman returns to his home and family. He pours out the whole story to his wife, and she actually predicts his downfall. By conquering sin and death, Jesus has already made a public show of Lucifer, breaking his power utterly. It remains for us, however, to "crush Satan under our feet". Where Jesus' feet have been, we may confidently look to put our feet. Philippians 4:13 encourages us also to be conquerors: "I can do everything through him who gives me strength." Let us be active in the service of our King, praying that he will bring an end to all evil and that we shall stand in the face of Satan's bitterness towards mankind. We need to thwart his plans wherever possible. We know that he is destined to hang on the same gallows which he has built for us. His end has already been secured.

Like Mordecai, we should not be looking for reward and blessing. In Luke 17:10 Jesus explains that even when we, as the Lord's servants, have done everything asked of us, we should still count ourselves unworthy servants. At best we have only done our duty. It is God's pleasure to bless our service for him, not because we have earned it, but because of his boundless love for us. We are told in 1 Peter to anticipate receiving a crown; thus God will honour us publicly. We'll not keep these crowns, however – we'll lay them all at Jesus' feet.

The blessings come thick and fast, and are unbelievable in their power and scope. In 2 Timothy 2 we are told that we shall reign with Jesus. We get to keep the King's own garment and horse – the signs of his authority. With everlasting life before us, a new song is on our lips – a song which only we, the redeemed, can sing. The prospect is overwhelming. Nevertheless, let us keep it all in its right proportions. The apostle John in Revelation 4 inspired Charles Wesley to write this wonderful hymn, so let these words spur us on to greater things:

Past Perfect

Changed from glory into glory,
Till in heaven we take our place;
Till we cast our crowns before thee,
Lost in wonder, love, and praise.

Read: Esther 6:1-14; 2 Timothy 2:8-13; Revelation 4:1-11.

Consider and pray: It does appear, at times, as if Satan is in control. But God has him on a lead. Just when he seems about to overrun us, the Lord turns his plotting back on his own head. The Lord never forgets the faithfulness of his servants, and in due time they will receive their reward. If you are suffering under the enemy's barrage, take courage from the stories of Mordecai and Esther and a host of other witnesses who have stood their ground and ultimately rejoiced in Satan's downfall. Do not fall into the trap of low self-esteem; false humility is as sinful as pride. We must see ourselves as God sees us – as kings and priests before him who are destined to rule and reign at his side.

30
No crying there!

He will wipe every tear from their eyes. There will be no more death or mourning or crying or pain, for the old order of things has passed away.

Revelation 21:4

At this very moment, you may be struggling with one or more of the things mentioned in this scripture. Your eyes may well be filled with tears from either physical or emotional pain. You may even be thinking and feeling that it's all very well for people to talk about healing, or prosperity, or any number of other blessings, but the truth is that you personally aren't experiencing any of them. Today we live in an instant world where you don't have to wait very long for anything. Take soup-in-a-cup, for example. Many years ago, I used to make soup – I mean from scratch! I started with a huge marrow bone, which my butcher would saw into three or four pieces. I took these home and stewed them until they had given up all their marrow and were hollow, and then I discarded them. What was left was my stock, around which I built my soup. It certainly took time to achieve the best results. These days I couldn't buy a marrow bone for my dogs from our local butcher – it would never get as far as his shop. I like to think that my soup was in a different league to the instant in-a-cup variety we get now.

You may not be absolutely thrilled at being likened to a bowl of soup, but I do believe that God is a "master" in everything he practises. Whilst at times he does seem to produce an instant, in-a-moment healing or an on-the-spot answer to prayer, it is not usually these things which draw the deepest treasures from our lives. Like my quality soup, this takes time and patience, with many ingredients and much striving. For many people the idea of long-term dealings with God is outside their experience and expectations. They feel that there must be something wrong if they're not always and immediately receiving blessing, so they dig around in themselves looking for the failure. Or they turn to other means in order to find relief. Or perhaps they even pretend that God has answered their request, although in reality nothing has changed at all.

Whilst it is not wrong to long for and cry out for instant answers, we must understand that our goal is not healing, or spiritual gifts, or material possessions, or even happiness – our goal is Jesus himself. He has all the answers, and when we meet with him face to face, there will be plenty of time to ask all our questions. We'll have all of eternity in which to discover why one person received their healing and the next one in line did not. I just wonder whether we'll really be interested in knowing then, because when you meet with Jesus everything else fades into insignificance. So, let us pray for health, comfort and our material needs, but let us not become preoccupied with them. Receiving these does not necessarily bring us closer to God.

No crying there!

If you are in physical pain, first of all seek Jesus. Then pray for healing and even accept the doctor's help. Let's use every means available; there is no merit in suffering pain unnecessarily. But please don't make the mistake that many do, of substituting the doctor for Jesus.

If you're grieving at the loss of someone you love, first of all seek Jesus. He may not bring the dead back to life, but in your sorrow, he just might become closer to you than he ever was before. Whatever you do, don't seek the dead themselves. This path leads to spiritualism, mediums and clairvoyants, into deception and away from God.

If you need hard cash, first of all seek Jesus. He may speak to you about changing your lifestyle and getting out of debt, but he'll not leave you comfortless and alone. You may not always like what Jesus says, but you'll never regret taking the advice he gives.

In the midst of all this seeking of Jesus, we will undoubtedly see mighty miracles and signs and healings. He may well even raise the dead or show you which fish has the coin hidden in it. But, even if that doesn't happen, he's still the same Jesus. He has promised never to leave us or forsake us. He will provide us with everything we need in order to live holy lives and get the job which he's given us to do completed. Meanwhile, we hold on to the promise that a day is coming when once and for all he will wipe away every tear. Death, mourning, crying and pain will be no more.

No longer will there be any curse. The throne of God and the Lamb will be in the city, and his servants will serve him. They will see his face, and his name will be on their foreheads. There will be no more night. They will not need the light of a lamp or the light of the sun, for the Lord God will give them light. And they will reign for ever and ever.

Revelation 22:3-5

Praise God that we are moving towards that day, and that when the deaf do hear, the blind see and the dead are raised, we are seeing glimpses of the reality of the kingdom. Let's continue to pray and work for this kingdom to come, that God's will may be done here and now on earth as it is in heaven!

Read: Revelation 21:1-5 & 22:1-7; Matthew 6:25-34.

Consider and pray: As we come to the close of our meditations, let us reevaluate our aims and objectives. Jesus himself is the only goal worthy of our time and effort. As we seek first him and his kingdom, so we shall find that all these other things will be added to us. And whatever life may deal out to us in the present, we are assured a future free from all curses – a future where our enemies and the enemies of God are never heard of again. "Amen. Come, Lord Jesus."

> *My goal is God himself, not joy, nor peace,*
> *Nor even blessing, but himself, my God:*
> *'Tis his to lead me there, not mine, but his –*
> *"At any cost, dear Lord, by any road!"*
>
> *So faith bounds forward to its goal in God,*
> *And love can trust her Lord to lead her there:*
> *Upheld by him, my soul is following hard,*
> *Till God hath full fulfilled my deepest prayer.*
>
> *No matter if the way be sometimes dark,*
> *No matter though the cost be oft-times great,*
> *He knoweth how I best shall reach the mark,*
> *The way that leads to him must needs be strait.*

No crying there!

One thing I know, I cannot say him nay;
One thing I do, I press towards my Lord;
My God, my glory here, from day to day,
And in the glory there my great reward.

F. Brook